MW01093093

Love Letters
to Miscarried Moms

Written in the midst of my grief so that
you will not be alone in yours.

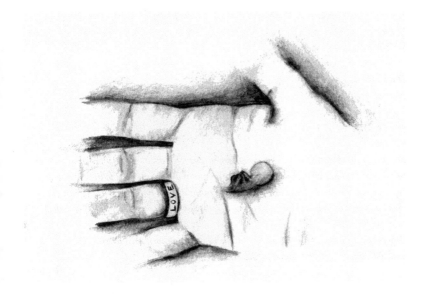

SAMANTHA EVANS

WESTBOW
PRESS
A DIVISION OF THOMAS NELSON

Cover Art By: Jorie Lee
Editor: Debra L. McGoldrick

WestBow Press books may be ordered through booksellers or by contacting:

WestBow Press
A Division of Thomas Nelson
1663 Liberty Drive
Bloomington, IN 47403
www.westbowpress.com
1-(866) 928-1240

ISBN: 978-1-4497-1002-6 (sc)
ISBN: 978-1-4497-1004-0 (hc)
ISBN: 978-1-4497-1003-3 (e)

Library of Congress Control Number: 2010942340

Printed in the United States of America

WestBow Press rev. date: 01/23/2012

To God the Father, who holds all saints, both in heaven
and on earth, in the palm of His all-powerful hand,

To the Lord Jesus Christ, who left His throne to walk beside me,

To the Holy Spirit, who spoke strength into my heart
as my fingers clicked this book into place,

To Clint, my knight, and the Lord's apprentice,

And to Grandma Lewis, who will be with Christ this Christmas.

December 14, 2010

Contents

Contents

Preface

I'm sorry, friend, I truly am. There are not words to describe the unfathomable pain you feel. And yet, for your sake, and for mine, I have to try. You see, just like you, I am a miscarried mother. The child was my first. And though I have no birth certificate, no war stories of labor and nothing left to show of my pregnancy, I know by the loss that I feel (I write this in the midst of my loss) from last Sunday that I am a mother.

I have memories of the first time I felt light-headed and the first time I noticed soreness under my ribs from when my body rearranged itself. I printed out all the first and second day congratulations that I received on Facebook. I have memories of the first person who prayed for my baby and the best congratulatory responses I received. The giddy ones were my favorite. There is the journal that I began writing to my unborn child and the pictures... Pictures of my pregnancy test and progress pictures from when I was convinced I was getting bigger, but no one else could tell.

Surreal. Devastating. How can I describe a pain that turned my heart inside out? I can't manage. There are not enough syllables or expletives in the English language, or in any language, for that matter. And so I am left with nothing more than I am sorry, so, so sorry.

I needed to know I wasn't alone. For two days I only wanted to speak to women who had miscarried. I am angry, still, at unfit mothers who get pregnant accidentally and then wish that their children hadn't been born. I can hardly speak to women who have not miscarried because their good fortune pulls me into tears—as if it takes any prompting.

The day after I miscarried I was journaling (therapeutically) and God laid the phrase "Love Letters to Miscarried Moms" on my heart. Immediately I knew that it was the title of a book. But, I did not decide to write the book myself. *Well, I guess I'm writing a book.* This felt somewhat ironic because the night that I miscarried I said, through screaming and crying and yelling, "I don't want to help other people who have gone through this! I don't want to have compassion on miscarried moms! I don't want this!"

I know you understand my grief. It wasn't that I didn't want to have empathy for you, miscarried mothers. I didn't want to *be* a miscarried mom at all. But, I think that even in the midst of my grief I knew that God would use this for His glory—to try to touch your heart. He loves you so much. He wants you to know that, and He does truly want what is best for you. And so I set out to write this book, and to interview others I knew who had gone through miscarriages as well.

I have included in the back a section called, "Helpful Tips on How to Manage the Grieving," just in case you are reading this book and haven't had a miscarriage; but rather, you are seeking insight as to what your miscarried mother friend is going through. If you are, thank you. I have also included, in an appendix, miniature biographies of each woman I interviewed. Maybe one of them will have a story similar to yours.

These are the women that have been my heroes through this process. I know that your story, your experience, was scary and horrific, but you are not alone. Grieve with us. Throw tantrums with us. Swear with us. As I said to my friend Sandie, "If you can't swear about the death of your child, then what can you swear about?" This isn't easy. This is the raw, uncut gruesome side of life that no one can possibly understand unless one has been there. We've been there.

It's safe to cry with us and to vent with us. If you choose to throw things with us, we'd prefer your projectiles were not aimed at people. We'll get through this together and, on the flipside of this cover, my hope and prayer is that you realize the inner strength that you have been given to find your way out of the dark and lonely forest of your grief—maybe even having gained a literary friend or two along the way.

All the women I talked with have different stories, but each woman said the same thing, "Allow yourself to grieve the loss." This book is my love letter to you. This book is the stories of women who have been where you are and know how you feel without you requiring the words to describe it.

I hope that reading this helps you cope with your grief the way that writing it has helped me cope with mine. Let's find our way out of this darkness together. Know that you are normal. You are one out of four pregnancies. You are not alone. You are loved.

Thursday, October 01, 2009

Sam I Am

Before I start talking to you about possibly the very worst day of your life, I thought I should introduce myself. As you read, you will quickly learn that it is hard for me to be anything but real—*all the time*. Which is why, when I was only three weeks along in my pregnancy, a gazillion people knew that I was pregnant—a very painful reality that haunted me the day I miscarried our first and only child thus far.

Sam. Just Sam. The name on the cover of this book is Samantha Evans because that's what the credit card companies like to go by, but for us, you and me, it's just Sam.

I was born and raised in Chicagoland. Chicagoland is not an actual city near Chicago, but the nickname for all surrounding suburbs. Also, for the record, Chicago was named the "Windy City" because of a long-winded politician, not actual wind, and there are no suburbs east of Chicago—just a lake. A very big lake. These are things that I feel compelled to clear up.

So, Chicagoland it is. I remember watching the '85 Bears with my dad—Walter Payton, Jim McMahon, Mike Ditka—the year they won the Super Bowl. I watched Jordan play and was amidst the chaos each of the six times the Chicago Bulls won the World Championship in the 90's. I wasn't actually at the stadium. I didn't need to be. The entire Chicagoland area went crazy.

1

Other than comments about *how windy* the Windy City is, the most frequent question people ask me about Chicago is whether I am a Cubs fan or a Sox fan (questions about traffic are a close third—all the stereotypes are true).

Since you didn't open this book to read about the Cubs-Sox rivalry—and if you aren't from Chicago you probably don't care—I'll spare you and continue. (And, in case you were wondering, this is me, intentionally avoiding the answer.)

I graduated from Naperville Central High School in '99 and went on to Northwestern College in St. Paul, MN where I majored in Youth Ministry and Bible. I had known since I was a sophomore in high school that God was calling me into youth ministry. I worked at CrossRoads Church in Lakeville, MN for two and a half years while I was going to school and played enough hours of Ultimate Frisbee to have majored in it—seriously.

I graduated in 2003 and that summer, at Sonshine, a Christian Woodstock, I met Clint Evans. Recognize the last name? Clint and I went on our first date together that Sunday: Applebees and *X-Men II*. We dated that summer and the entire time I kept saying, "We can't get serious," "We can't get serious," because I knew that I was moving back to Chicago at the end of the summer. Now we're married. The man is persistent, what can I say? That, and God has a sense of humor. He and I have a certain *understanding* about things. I tell God what I refuse to do and then He laughs at the absurdity of my giving Him ultimatums. However, despite my incessant protest I am always blessed in the end when things happen God's way.

I was once planning a trip to visit my mom for the same week she was planning on being gone on a motorcycle trip. Communication is not our forte. Her trip was cancelled, which was hooray for me. She said, "So Samantha," (my family calls me that. They've also turned my name into only two syllables: Sman-tha over the years). "So Smantha, I hope you didn't pray for that to happen." My reply was, "I don't have to pray, Mom. God and I just have an understanding."

People also seem to think that I have a better standing with God because I am a youth minister. Not true. They don't understand our understanding. I love my family to pieces; we're pretty tight,

I'd say—even the cousins—and *I told God* that I was never going to move away from home. Now I'm living in Oregon, two thousand miles from home. I *also* told God that I would never work in a Lutheran church—their liturgical services are just not my first worship style choice and, overall, they tend to be more liberal than I am. I moved to Oregon to work at a Lutheran Church.

But remember the blessings I talked about? All the Lutherans I have met are pretty darn nice. They *definitely* know how to potluck, which I have just turned into a verb. I'm now convinced that potlucks are a cross-denominational talent. The two things we all have in common: Christ and potlucks. It should really be that simple.

I *also* told God that I would *never* be a pastor's wife. I just didn't want that call. You already know the punch line to this joke. This year Clint came home from school and said that God has *not* called him to be a counselor, which is what he originally thought; God has called him to be a *pastor*. Yeah, thanks for that. Good supportive wife that I am, I tried to convince Clint that he was wrong.

Clint. He is a sentence in and of himself and if you knew him you'd understand. Clint was a drug addict and alcoholic before the legal drinking age. While many twenty-one year olds are going out to buy their first legal drink, Clint was checking himself into Teen Challenge, a Christian rehab facility. His first week in there, God knocked him upside the head with a spiritually-sized 2X4, which is what it takes to get Clint's attention sometimes. Now, seven years and a pastor's heart later, he is actually working at a Teen Challenge facility. He supervises the guys there.

Two years ago Clint got a tattoo on each forearm that spells out "Prodigal Son." The story is recorded in Luke 15 if you'd like to take a look at it, but it is essentially Clint's story. He ran away from God but then found his way back again. Last year he shaved his head and this year he started playing semi-pro football and bulked up quite a bit. He recently grew a mustache and goatee. No complaints here, but my point is this: My husband looks more and more like a skinhead all the time. Some of the sweet, little, old ladies at our church are scared to talk to him, which he doesn't really like very much. Every once in awhile he gets profiled and shadowed by a police officer—I've seen it happen. He doesn't like that, either. However, often times, teenagers (and sometimes grown men) who pass him on the street look terrified—this, Clint thinks is funny.

The really wonderful thing, though, is that while words like "strong" and "tough" are used to describe my husband, words like "adorable" and "teddy-bear" are used just as frequently. He'll try to tell you that he's an idiot, but don't listen to him, he is an idiot—because he is *incredibly* smart, especially with people. This summer he read philosophy books just for fun. I tried to tell him that idiots don't read philosophy books just for fun, but he wouldn't listen—because he's an idiot. Where's that 2X4 when you need it?

Clint and I got married one week short of twenty-three…for both of us. He's only four days older than me. I used to say that I wanted my husband to be older than me but not too much older. After I met him I called my sister, Jorie, and said, "His birthday is April 2nd."

She replied, "Well, that's older, but not too much older."

Clint has always been convinced that we are going to raise all "little line-backers." When we found out we were pregnant he declared, "My child is going to be a man mountain of awesomeness," (It's a Brian Urlacher [Chicago Bear] commercial). Then he added, "even if it's a girl." I had this awful image of my daughter coming out with a full goatee.

I must also add that Clint is a Vikings fan. I asked his brother Darry, "What do you get when you cross a Bears fan with a Vikings fan?"

"I don't know. What?" He asked.

"I don't know," I replied. "I was hoping you could tell me. I guess we'll find out in May." We're not going to find out in May after all, but if you have a quippy answer, let me know. I have faith that it will happen one day.

Everyone's story is different. And even though as I write this I am on the verge of tears, I will share my story, and the stories of other women that I know with you because I want you to know that you are not alone.

In May, Clint and I decided that the pack of pills that would bring me through the end of July would be our last. From May through the first half of August I nearly went crazy trying to keep our secret. Well, alright, so I told one friend—but only one—Emily. I had to tell *someone.* July 26th was my last pill, July 30th, the first day of my last period. I was pregnant within ten days. Sometimes it feels like it didn't really happen at all.

The Plus Sign or the Double Line

Pregnancy Excitement

All pregnancies begin the same way—with, what I like to call "the fun part." When I stopped the pill at the beginning of August my hormones went through the roof and I started chasing my husband around the house—literally—not that he ever put up much of a fight...

We'd been to the doctor in July and I was checked out for possible hereditary challenges. My friend Emily (the one friend who knew) was on stand-by—for what I wasn't sure, but she was there if I needed her. Then we stopped the pill. It was real now. And though, sometimes while I was on my back, I thought, *we could be making a baby right now*, sex never became a chore. We didn't have time for it to be.

Following the miscarriage, whenever I get to the only-ten-days-off-the-pill part of my story everyone says, "Oh, you'll have no trouble getting pregnant again." We'll see. No one can say for sure.

Maybe your story varies from mine here. Maybe getting pregnant was not so easy for you. Maybe, like my cousin, Jenny, who is in her late thirties, you were trying a year *before* you miscarried. It has been two years since and still nothing is happening. My friend Misty miscarried and it was two years for her before her son Steven was conceived. Steven is twenty-eight now and has two younger brothers, also in their twenties. Though Misty's loss happened three decades ago, the pain has left a vivid scar upon her memory.

Or maybe, like my friend Sandie or my Aunt Diane, you have had multiple still-births and have never carried a child until full term. Maybe pregnancy isn't exciting at all for you, but terrifying. Grief keeps digging a bigger hole and you're not sure if you can crawl out. You're not even sure if you want to.

I have no magical cure for miscarriages. Miscarriages are the unfortunate result of living in an imperfect world. The entire process, though, has caused me to value life so much more. The process of getting pregnant and forming a baby is so miraculous. I have to pause to think of all the intricate details that have to line up just perfectly. In my mind it makes Psalm 139 so much more substantial as the Psalmist declares, "For you created my inmost being. You knit me together in my mother's womb. I praise you because I am fearfully and wonderfully made. Your works are wonderful; I know that full well." Wonderful is exactly what it was—at first.

I had never been pregnant before and did not know what it felt like to be pregnant, but I had a *very* strong suspicion that I was during what I believe was only the second week. This may sound egotistical to you, and I don't mean for it to. I have had a six-pack since I was twelve. Huge thighs, thin scraggly hair, but my abdominal muscles are the part of my body in which I have always taken pride. Even after hardcore core workouts I rarely get sore. But then on September 1st my abs were still extremely tender a couple of days after a medium level abdominal workout. Thoughts flew through my head like, *Maybe I need to be working out more* or *Maybe it's just because I'm getting older*. Another huge clue for me was that same morning, when I got back from my run, my nipples were purple. All this time I had just thought "purple nurples" were a myth, but no, no, *they were real*. Initially the sight was somewhat shocking. A deep breath later I said out loud, "Well, *that's* not normal."

September 2nd-5th I became more aware of other small changes. (I only "remember" these dates because I journaled the happenings.) My belly button itched off and on and it was shaped differently. I know this because every so often I feel my belly button and over the years I have become very accustomed to its shape. I'm ridiculous. I know this. (Clint also reminds me all the time just in case I forget.) I found out for the first time that the infamous "pregnant glow" is really just a nice way of saying "oily and sometimes zitty face." I felt as if my abs were being pushed up and out, similar to Wolverine gently prying them back like a zipper.

My friend, Dia, noticed my oily and somewhat zitty face and called it the glow. She asked if I was late and my answer was "possibly." My cycle off the pill was always more stretched out then my cycle with the pill so according to my pill period schedule I was twelve days late. However, according to my off-the-pill period schedule I was only six days late. Since I hadn't had a "normal" period off of the pill I wasn't really sure what normal was.

The next day, September 6th I saw Emily at church and during our adult Bible study I whispered, "I'm six days late" and then walked away. I was scolded later for sharing such news and leaving it at that.

"Go home and take the test and put me out of my misery!"

"Doesn't it have to be the first pee of the day?"

"No!"

"Don't you have to wait a few weeks?"

"No! Go take the test."

Three years ago I'd skipped a period. It was a little awkward purchasing birth control and a pregnancy test in the same transaction but I still had one of the tests in a package from back then. I'd been saving it all this time for the perfect moment. So I peed on the stick with my husband eagerly waiting outside the bathroom door. I called Emily to tell her that, in fact, there was a little plus sign in the window.

As I mentioned earlier, I began a pregnancy journal. I was so excited about the idea of becoming a mother and I could not wait nine months to start telling my child how much it was loved.

September 16, 2009: It's just you and me until May and I wanted to take advantage of this time we have alone together.

I want to share with you things that I experience. Things that people say, and things that I am thinking and praying. Some of the things you'll probably wish you could forget, but this journal is for me, too. Other things I tell you I pray that you will always cherish. Here's to me and you. Here's to the love that we'll know from each other and here's to the LORD. It is He who has given us such a wonderful gift to share.

I love you, Sweetheart.
~Mom

I will share more of my pregnancy journal entries as we go along. They are bittersweet for me to reread but important for me to remember because they are part of my story. And, whereas now I can only look back, my journal entries were written as I experienced that part of my life. The descriptions are more vivid and fresh than my memory ever will be. I was really pregnant. I really did have a child growing inside me. I really am a mother who lost her child. And even though there is nothing to show for it anymore, the experience changed my life. It changed who I am and there is no going back.

Wait. Did That Just Happen?

Dia had three miscarriages after her second daughter was born. Before she knew anything was wrong with what turned out to be the third miscarriage, her oldest daughter, Iollia, who was five at the time, had a dream "that her brothers died." The next morning Dia started bleeding.

"Mommy, why did God take my brothers?" Iollia asked Dia.

Because God needed them up in heaven more than we needed them down here," she responded.

Dia told me that story to remind me that my baby was real and in really good hands. She also said something to me that I will never forget. "If we hadn't lost that baby, we never would have had Malinna." Malinna is such a precious gift to their family. Dia will never forget the children that she's lost but she has faith that God knows what He's doing.

There is a quote that I wrote on the inside of one of my photo albums in high school: "Don't cry because it's over. Smile because it happened." We're not there yet. We *are* still grieving our loss, but my goal is eventually to be able to "smile because it happened." Our children are real. They will never experience pain or heartbreak and I truly believe that right now they are playing up in heaven together, eagerly waiting until the day they get to greet us. They are only in heaven because they lived with us down here on earth.

Lona, whose fourth and fifth children were twins, and Sandie, who had one set of twins and two other pregnancies to follow, were able to rattle off the ages of their unborn children without a second thought. Their children are real. I will celebrate each moment that I had with my child. That's what my journal entries and this book have become…a celebration.

Looking back then (when I found out that I was pregnant) other details began to fall into place. The following italicized portions are several of my journal entries from that time.

August 14th: I went for a bike ride with [my friend], Barb. After only six miles on a semi-hot day I felt light-headed and was extremely *thirsty—but couldn't figure out why.*

August 20th: Went waterskiing and did a zipline with teenagers, so if your head is shaped funny, you know why. Earlier that day I shared with Kyle, the youth pastor at the Nazarene church here in town, that I was having trouble focusing. Thought it was because I'd had such a busy summer. Turns out there was more to it than that. ☺

August 27th: Had a very strong feeling and a voice in the back of my head telling me not to give blood. Clint insisted that I was being ridiculous. We weren't pregnant. He wasn't ready for me to be pregnant. Then he gave me a hug. "I know you're excited, Baby. It'll happen." Ha ha.

Written September 17, 2009: September 6th was the first day that I found out you were real. Off the pill ten days and then

*there you are. I went home from church and took the test. AJ
and Nick, two of our youth group boys, were at our house that
day. Nick was the first person to ever pray for you.*

I immediately texted pictures of the pregnancy test to my sisters
and two of my closest friends. My friend Alecia called and asked
what it was. When I told her that she was going to be an auntie she
screamed and squealed with me just like I'd hoped she would. Alecia
was an *excellent* first person to talk to.

While I was on the phone with Alecia, my sister Meredith sent a text
back saying, "Is this real? I'm going to be an aunt?"

A lot of people didn't answer right away. Figures. I called my friend
Carolyn twice and left a message once. When she called...
    "Hey, Care."
    "Are you pregnant?" She knew because I called twice and left a
message once.

When my dad finally called back he happened to be with my sister
Jorie.

"Dad, are you ready to be a Grandpa?"
    "What, Smantha, really?"
    "Yeah, Dad. I'm pregnant."
    "Congratulations! Was this planned?"
    "Yes."

"Was this planned?" Has been the number one question. Like I said,
Emily was the only one who knew. People tend to ask for progress
reports when they know that you're trying to have a baby. That's no
one else's business.

When Jorie got in the car, Dad handed her the phone and I told her
to look at the text that I had sent.
    "Smantha, really? Congratulations! Was this planned?" It began
to work itself out like a skit...
    "Yes. But we didn't have to wait long. I was only off the pill ten
days."

"Wow. That's fast."

"Yeah, Clint has super sperm."

"Apparently." At this point I was sitting at the dining room table with AJ and Nick, and Nick, poor freshman, choked on his noodles.

"Are you finished eating, Nick," his brother asked. Oops.

My cousin Debi's voicemail had my favorite variation of "Was this planned?" Following a text that I sent her saying, "Umm…Going to be a bit bigger for your wedding" (I am one of her bridesmaids), she left me an appropriate voicemail message.

"Was this planned or were you just being sneaky because I saw you two months ago and you didn't say a word [a lot more words that went by too fast for me to understand…] This will, of course, have to go in our book." Debi and I are writing a novel together.

I called Debi back and said, "It was planned, but we didn't have to wait long. I was only off the pill ten days. Told Jorie that Clint had super sperm. Said it right in front of one of my freshman. Poor boy couldn't finish his lunch." She laughed loudly. That became my favorite answer to the most frequently asked question.

I'll wager you also have witty stories about discovering that you were pregnant. Don't be afraid to laugh at the memories. Don't be afraid to make room for the baby in your heart the way that your body was making room for him or her right smack on top of your bladder. Your body was really changing because the baby was really there. You are a mother who lost her child.

When I called Emily the night that I miscarried, one of the first things I worried about was telling *all* the people that I had told I *was* pregnant, that I *wasn't* pregnant anymore. Before we ever knew about the miscarriage she said, "Sam, I don't know if I agree with waiting until the second trimester to tell people. If something does happen, you'll want people to know." She reiterated that same truth to me that night and then reassured me that I did not even have to think about telling people.

I had no idea how women could keep that secret for so long. In the days immediately following our miscarriage I voiced to Clint that

I wished we had waited to say something. Our loss was embarrassing and I somehow felt as if I'd let family members down. Clint looked at me, smiled and said, "No, Sweetie, you were *so* happy."

If, like me, you've told a million people that you're pregnant and now you feel like you have to tell a million people that you're not, don't worry. Call a couple key people and let them pass the news along. Also, depending on how you feel, ask them to, as they share the news, also mention that you would prefer no phone calls. Don't feel guilty at all about putting the caller ID on your cell phone to good use. If you don't feel like talking, then don't. Your friends will understand. If they don't, you should consider getting new friends.

Like Jenny said, "Really hard things happen to people that change who they are. It's a really personal journey," so I will not dictate how things have to be done.

But I will say this: share your story. If, like me, you're a talker, this is not as much a challenge for you, but if you're the type of person that keeps things to yourself it will be difficult. Even if you don't want to tell other people, find a cat or a dog, a journal, or babysit the infant of a close friend—who will not fear your running across state lines with her child—and talk it out. Own your story. Let it be real to you. Don't be afraid to grieve, to hurt, but celebrate the life that you had inside of you, Mommy.

September 7, 2009: Your dad and I went on a seven-mile hike at Silver Creek Falls to celebrate. Got a little light-headed once or twice.

September 8, 2009: I told council that I was pregnant. They cheered. Pastor Jeff prayed for you, "That their baby would be full of energy and life—which I don't think will be much of a problem considering its parents."

September 20, 2009: I don't really feel pregnant anymore. Haven't for a few days. I told Dia that I was scared that I was going to go to the doctor and they'd tell me I was wrong. She reassured me that that was normal; told me she'd felt the same way with Nada and Malinna. I guess it's normal for pregnant *women to have crazy dreams too. September 12th I dreamed that I was giving birth to a banana slug. Never should have looked at the four-week pictures. You looked like a big sluggish clump of cells.*

Everyone has been asking me if I've gotten sick. When I say, "no" they stare at me in awe; so thank you for that. I like low maintenance. When I have a girl, God is going to mold her into a high maintenance princess. ☺

Love you, can't stop writing but I have to. Have to be in church in twenty minutes and it's a ten minute drive. Oops.

Monday, September 21, 2009: Well, it's official. You're official, I should say. Went to the doctor's office and peed in a cup so they could tell me what I already knew—that I'm pregnant. It did feel good to get the confirmation, though. Wow. I'm pregnant. Can't believe it.

Saturday, September 26, 2009: The months that I have until I meet you are going so slow. I want to speed through time.

PS: If you're a girl, your father is going to spoil you rotten and keep you hidden away from the world at all costs. If you're a boy, get ready to hit the ground running.

Don't pretend that it didn't happen. It wasn't just a fetus or a clump of cells. It was your child. Celebrate that. Memorialize that however you know how. Will it hurt? Heck yeah. Some of what I wrote in my journal actually had a prophetic feel to it, as if God was helping me foreshadow what was about to happen. However, if you make the most of it and cherish the time that you had, then maybe in the future you'll be able to think back to memories of your child with fondness…and smile because it happened.

The No Good Very Bad Most Terrible Day

This chapter is really graphic, in my opinion, so if you'd rather not read about my vagina or clumps of blood, you'd best be moving on to the next chapter. I have included these details for women who've miscarried so they know they aren't alone in what I believe to be one of the most painful, horrific, grotesque events a human being can ever experience. If you choose to read on...well, at least you've been warned.

September 28, 2009: I'm not pregnant anymore...Brown spotting turned into pink into red...darker red to thicker.

The spotting began in church Sunday morning and continued throughout the day. I ended up having to put a pad in at 3:00 PM. I tried not to worry about the blood. Having never been pregnant before, maybe it was normal? But hope waned with the daylight. After youth group Sunday night, around 9:00, Clint and I were watching a movie and the cramps kicked in. And my heating pad, though effective at first, got restless and decided she'd rather lie between my legs. There were only a few steps on my abdomen before Ashley, our cat, settled in her new position.

Friends, with futile attempts to make me feel better that Sunday, kept telling me that miscarriage cramps were worse than any PMS cramps I could ever experience. These friends didn't know me in high school. In high school, the nurses used to see me once a month. I remember one of them getting angry and nearly shouting at me, "Why don't you take something for it!" This nurse did not understand that there was only about a thirty second window in which Ibuprofen would be of any use to me. There are sixty-second cars. I had sixty-second cramps—zero, zilch to full-blown, turn-your-uterus-inside-out cramps.

My sisters knew that if they saw my backpack in the foyer when they got home from school, if I was home before them, not to say a word to the sleeping bear upstairs. My miscarriage cramps felt no different than the days before high school and college, before I was on the pill, an invention for which God deserves my deepest heartfelt gratitude.

> *(Sept. 28th Continued) I had awful cramps so I got into the bathtub. The hot water made the pain go away completely. Just when I thought that my fears were all in my head, I queeffed and passed a quarter-sized clump of blood. I picked up the blood (never a good sign) as if it were a solid and stared at the glob in my hand.*

> *I don't know how many mothers who miscarry have the same opportunity, but I wish they all did. The word "closure" comes to mind. I saw it and then I had to look again. Head, lighter in shade, arms and legs tucked together in fetal position, I was staring at my baby—so anxious for life that he came out eight months too soon. The moment was sad and sweet at the same time. I held it. I stared at it. I was fascinated that what I was looking at most people would only be able to see in a picture. I was fascinated that it was my child, mine and Clint's, and that God had formed it inside of me. I wear the purity ring that my father gave me in college on my right hand now, to set an example for the teens in my youth group. The phrase "True Love Waits" took on a whole new meaning as I stared at the baby in my right hand.*

It took a few tries for sound to come out when I called for Clint to come. I showed it to him. To this day he wishes that he hadn't seen it. We put it in a plastic bag and put it in the fridge to bring to the doctor. Don't know why—it seemed appropriate at the time. Maybe the doctor could give me a reason.

I emptied the bathwater and began to shower the blood off myself. As I showered, a larger clump of blood came out proceeded by a cramp-contraction. All of a sudden I had another. The shape and movement my abdomen made involuntarily seemed cartoon-esque to me. However, that amazement ended quickly when I saw what followed. I had passed the placenta-in-forming and it was about the size of a sixteen-inch softball until it splat flat on the floor of the tub.

It's 3 AM. If it was raining I would so turn on Matchbox Twenty right now. I'm so tired.

After that grotesque amount of blood was expelled the discharges got smaller and smaller. I went to the bathroom three times just before bed and once more just now, each time discharging smaller amounts of blood. I have seen so much blood in the last fifteen hours that toward the end of my shower yesterday I was kicking the clumps down the drain in tears. "Alright, alright," I screamed out loud. "I get it! I'm not pregnant anymore!"

That's when it hit. For three weeks I've been saying, "I'm pregnant," with giddy glee. This time I held my stomach and said, "I'm not pregnant anymore!" Tears started flowing. I started sobbing and couldn't stop. Unbeknownst to me, Clint was sitting in the bathroom the whole time, listening. He was there and "dead inside" as I screamed, "Yes! …What the hell *does that mean!?"*

You see…

I just realized that this "you see" was the pivotal moment in my writing wherein I stopped writing for myself and began writing for you, miscarried mothers. Man, God is so *sneaky.*

You see, in the middle of my crying God caught me off guard with the most absurd question: "Are you ready to be blessed now?" That's how I know it was God the Father—because that man is crazy and rarely ever makes sense to me. I didn't answer. I was too angry. He repeated (doesn't like being ignored), "Are you ready to be blessed?"

"Yes!" I screamed. "But what the hell *does that mean?"*

I don't usually answer God out loud but it made Him feel more real in that moment and I needed God to feel real.

After my shower I cried uncontrollably. Pad in to catch the lighter bleeding with a few trips to the toilet to catch the heavier stuff that I could tell was coming each time. It was like a sneeze of the vagina.

Clint kept hearing the words "more blood," "more blood," and was begging to take me to the ER. You may be wondering why in the world I didn't go to the ER, if you're not already wondering why you chose to read this journal entry.

I warned you.

When I had started spotting on Sunday, I planned on going into the doctor's office first thing Monday morning. I have heard horror stories of women miscarrying, not knowing it, and having all the garbage that I discharged still stuck inside of them and causing infection. As for me, I recognized that my body was cleaning itself out. And why go to the ER? There is nothing a doctor or anyone else can do to prevent a miscarriage in the first trimester or stop it from happening once the process has already begun. As for the abdominal cramps and period quantity bleeding, that can wait until tomorrow's doctor's visit.

Right now I am just going to fall asleep next to Clint, for the second time tonight. He's fallen asleep with his ESPN magazine still upright in his hands and ready to read. What a roller coaster ride this has been. How awful! I'm too tired to focus. Good night, world. I'll see you again tomorrow.

I remember writing that last sentence as if to assure you and myself that I would not be committing suicide that evening. I'm not suicidal, but the thought of a peaceful death definitely crossed my mind. No, I have too much to live for and so I will continue on, even though nothing will ever be the same.

I guess, looking back, there are certain things for which I am grateful. I am grateful that it happened quickly. I am unsure of how long before the expulsion our baby died, but from the time that I started bleeding until the time I passed the largest clump of blood, only twelve hours passed. I'm grateful that not only was I at home, but in my bathtub, the easiest place for the process to take place. I am grateful that I got to see the baby. I am grateful that Clint was with me. I am also grateful for the words, "Are you ready to be blessed now?" even though I have no idea what they mean yet. Also, when I *do* go into labor I will spend half of my labor in a hot tub and the other half either walking around the room or bouncing on one of those huge balls. I understand that a baby at full-term is going to be bigger and slightly more painful to pass through, but heat and gravity will be close friends of mine. Dr. Mary can catch my child with a net.

Stay positive. Do your best. The no good, very bad, most terrible day will always be just that, but sorrow will swallow us up if we let it. Keep fighting. Fight to find your smile again. I don't know the details of your miscarriage, but I do know this, and maybe you and I have this in common: the thing that I am most grateful for with the miscarriage— is that it's over.

The Doctor's Visit

The very next morning Clint and I went to the doctor's office together. I was still in shock and wondered if the night before had not been more than a vivid nightmare. But sitting in the exam room atop the loud, crinkly wax paper, the loss became real and I fought to hold back the tears as I explained to Dr. Mary the particulars of what had happened the night before. I hated hearing her confirm that I'd had a miscarriage. That made it real, too.

Because the visit to the doctor's office was such an emotional part of my experience, it was one of the things that I asked other miscarried mothers about. It's amazing how much that initial hospital visit can be a catalyst for either pain or peace.

As hard as it was to keep Grandma on task when it came to answering questions (I say this with the most gentle and endearing heart), there are some memories that are just as dramatic to her as if they happened yesterday. She was between two and three months along for each of her miscarriages. She told me how for one of them her doctor, a "big guy," when he got to the room, was out of breath because he had run up the steps in a hurry to see my grandma. His urgency must have meant a great deal to her because more than sixty years later she still remembers it.

I truly hope that your doctor has cared for you through this process and has been kind and sympathetic and understanding, not at all like my friend Erica's, whom she referred to as "a butthead."

Erica had started bleeding so she went into the hospital. She was on the pill, so pregnancy was the furthest thing from her mind. Her doctor's statement to her was, "You were pregnant." Poor Erica found out in the same breath that she was pregnant and had lost the baby.

When my Aunt Diane got to the hospital the orderly behind the counter was more concerned about the paperwork than the fact that my aunt had blood dripping down her leg. Recalling the anger that she felt toward that nurse my aunt said, "I'm bleeding all over the place and you want my friggin' insurance? We've got bigger problems than that, Lady, you know?"

Later the same orderly tried to get her to calm down and said, "Oh, you can have another one."

It's hard. It's so hard. People who haven't experienced a miscarriage just—don't—know. I can't imagine that they are intentionally rude or insensitive; they simply cannot comprehend what you and I have been through. And our pain is so acute that it may as well be our hearts bleeding. Calloused comments hit our open wounds like daggers.

It's good to spend a little time talking about the doctor's office because most of us have gone through the same follow-up procedure for a child that is no longer in our womb…and that sucks. I went to the doctor's office once when I was first pregnant, peed in a cup so they could confirm that I was pregnant and then two weeks later had my blood drawn so they could check my hormone levels because I was no longer pregnant. Freak! (That's sometimes what I say when I get frustrated.)

I am making no claims to be an expert. I tried to Google DNC on the internet and my computer asked, "Did you mean D&C?" I really hate being outsmarted by the computer. One of the questions that many people asked me after I miscarried was whether or not I was going to have to have a D&C.

A D&C (Dilation and Curettage) is a process that scrapes the uterus clean to ensure that there is nothing left after a miscarriage that would cause infection or harm to the mother. You may not have had to have this procedure done. I didn't. About half of miscarriages that happen before ten weeks happen naturally and a D&C is not needed. The chance of the necessity of a D&C becomes more likely after the first ten weeks.

I wish I had known more about D&C's as I talked to women that I knew. Because I'd had a chance to see my baby that was one of the questions I asked each mother. However, for women who had to have a D&C, their babies did not necessarily come out in one piece. As my Aunt Diane so gently put it, "they basically vacuumed the baby out."

If the baby is at four to five months, women typically have to have induced labor and then a D&C to boot. Lona said that they brought her to the maternity ward for her induced labor. She could hear women in labor and babies crying. There were pictures and posters on the wall and everywhere she looked reminders pointed at her misfortune with a mocking finger.

Was this you? Or maybe I'm freaking you out because you might need to have one done. I'm sorry. Nothing about a miscarriage is clean or neat or heart-warming. Nothing anyone can say can clear away the black clouds and replace them with rainbows and unicorns. If you have to have a D&C, ask to be knocked out. From what others have said you do not want to be awake for the process. It is an unfortunate reality, a necessary evil. More than one woman I talked to said that it's essentially like having an abortion.

I don't know what your hospital experience was like. Whether good or bad, the fact that you do not have a baby inside of you anymore is a hard reality to grasp. I wasn't sure if my heart would survive that pain and if it could, I wasn't sure how I would manage. I will. I have to. You will, too. Life keeps going and so must we. In case you had a really crumby doctor's visit experience, here is mine. Erase yours and make this your new reality. I don't mind sharing, as you may have noticed.

My doctor really encouraged me. She never brought up the acronym D&C. After I described the horrific events that transpired she said, "I think you'd be surprised at the number of women who have miscarried." She raised her hand. I was taken aback. Was she saying that women will volunteer that information or that *she* was volunteering that information?

"Have *you* had a miscarriage?"

"Yes. It was my first pregnancy, like you."

"And you were able to have children without any problem after that?"

"Yes."

Dr. Mary is new to Lebanon, new to the Park Street clinic and the only family doctor/ OBGYN at that clinic, which happens to be only four blocks from my house. When Clint and I looked for a doctor back in July, she was the first name we came across. And then, sitting in the exam room with her, I learned that she, too, had had a miscarriage. It wasn't something to boast about or be grateful for; however, it is comforting to know that not only is my doctor a savvy expert about what I am going through physically, she also knows what I am going through emotionally because she has experienced it too.

"One out of five pregnancies ends in miscarriage and most of them, by far, happen in the first trimester," she assured me.

"Why is that?"

"Up until eleven or twelve weeks everything is still forming, developing. So, if something is wrong, wrong with the DNA, the wrong number of chromosomes or something's off with miosis/ mitosis...you know about that right?"

"Yeah."

"Than that would cause problems sooner rather than later."

"What is the percentage of miscarriages that happen after the first trimester?"

"I'd say one in a thousand."

"Why does it go down so much?"

"Because at twelve weeks, sometimes you get lucky at eleven, when you hear the heartbeat, then from that point on the baby is already fully developed and just continuing to grow."

"Does my miscarriage make me more susceptible to them in the future?"

"Not at all. I wouldn't start worrying [about you] until the third miscarriage."

She was so patient and so helpful, but the relief I felt with that statement was quickly shrouded by my heart falling into my stomach. I don't know that my heart could handle another miscarriage. Fear will cloud reason from time to time and this fear was new, unprecedented and unfathomable. What if I could not carry a child to full term?

When I shared this fear with my Aunt Mary she said, "Those are just fears you have to leave with the Lord." And she was right. There is nothing I can do about it either way.

Despite my fear and my shaking disposition, I left the doctor's office grateful for a visit that I believed had gone absolutely as well as possible considering the circumstances.

I left the doctor's office with her warning:

"You will continue bleeding for at least a week." I also left the doctor's office with the following instructions:

<u>No sex for a week or two</u> (until I had stopped bleeding completely). This would not be a problem because for five days following, my sex drive was null and void. Even Clint made some suggestive remarks about his *lack* of sex drive after everything that had taken place.

<u>No trying again until I had at least one normal period.</u> Again, at the time, at least, I didn't think that would be a problem. I developed a short-term fear of sex as well. (After a few days, hormones trumped fear). I was afraid to have sex again because I was afraid to get pregnant again, but I was also afraid of not getting pregnant again. I was also afraid that the intimacy that takes place during sex would be a really, cruel, painful reminder that I wasn't pregnant anymore and that I had lost my child. I was right.

I left the doctor's office with her reassurance. "There was *nothing* that you could have done to cause it—not exercise, not food, not sex, it was nothing *you* did." And, "There was nothing doctors could have done to stop it."

Most importantly, though, I left the doctor's office with hope, which is the greatest gift that my optimistic heart will ever receive.

The Aftermath

Miscarriage is not really a popular topic of conversation. Before two weeks ago I can only ever remember people saying, "Oh, so and so had a miscarriage." Frowny face.

"Oh! That's too bad. I think so and so did too."

"Oh, sad."

"Sad!"

End conversation, new topic. Miscarriage is something that happens to someone else. The few times that people have mentioned their miscarriages to me I have been guilty of the same thing. "Oh, that's too bad." Never, ever could I have come close to fathoming the weighted grief behind those words—that to a mother it meant the loss of a child. People always say, "Mommy-to-be" and "Daddy-to-be." Out of sight out of mind. Could not even fathom...

The word miscarriage really moves the conversation along. For instance, today two Latter Day Saints men came to my door. First of all, the rapping on the door scared the living daylights out of me. When I start typing on the keyboard I get tunnel vision and the knock startled me back to consciousness. They asked how I was doing and I was completely honest.

"I'm not doing so well, actually," I admitted not-so-sheepishly. "I just had a miscarriage and I'm writing about it. To be honest, I don't really feel like talking right now. But thank you so much for stopping by."

At the word miscarriage the one dropped his head but then quickly recovered. "Is there anything we can do for you?"

"Maybe just pray for me as you walk to the next house? I'd appreciate it."

People don't know what to say. They don't know how to respond. As my Aunt Diane said, "People try to say the right things…"

I continued, "But their words fall so short…"

"Because there is nothing anyone can say," she finished.

Jenny said that after hers she didn't want anything to do with anyone who hadn't been through it. People say really dumb things. I had one guy say, "Well, I guess God changed His mind, huh?" My advice to you is this. Take a deep breath. They mean well and you have bigger things to worry about—like fixing the hole in your heart. Don't feel guilty for being mad at them for never having gone through this. But go talk to someone who has.

The day after, I felt as if life had been sucked out of me. Before and after the doctor's appointment I spent a great deal of time on the phone, calling back the few mother-friends I had been on the phone with throughout the day before. I had to tell them that our worst fears had been realized. Everything was *not* okay. I had had a miscarriage.

"I'm going to go burn things," I said to Clint, not putting much effort into my sentence structure. A more accurate and complete thought would have been, "Hey Clint, I'm going to go out to the backyard and burn some of our yard debris in our fire pit because it will give me something to do and staring into a fire seems like it would be really tranquil and comforting right now." But who has the effort to explain complete thoughts? So, "I'm going to burn things," was good enough for me.

My cousin, Angela, with whom I was on the phone, laughed at me and I ended up having to fill in some blanks for her anyway. Things were going great until I dropped my phone into the fire. The keypad is now bubbly and shiny and it takes a lot more force of the thumb to text. The screen has tiny cracks all over it but none of them penetrated—everything still works just fine and today, three weeks later, I'm still using the same phone.

There is a reason I'm telling you this story and it's not just to say that my teenagers laugh at me for it...as if they needed any more ammo. The phone, nearly every time I look at it, reminds me of the day after my miscarriage. Also, it looks a lot like me. It is cracked and some things on it are broken but nothing necessary for it to function properly—it just takes a little more effort to get it to work. And, I was sure that the flap over the charger slot would have been melted to the phone or the charger itself been broken—one more battery cycle and then the phone is through, but I was wrong. The phone can still be recharged, just like me.

When the teens ask me why I don't just get a *new* phone (they don't understand because they get a small scratch and they're out the door to the store) I simply say, "Because it still works," and then I smile. And they laugh at me. And their train of thought moves so lighting-quick away from that morning-after-the-miscarriage moment outside by my fire pit that, that without even trying, without even knowing it, they pull me out of my grief as if they were pulling *me* out of the fire.

My T-shirt from the 2007 Spring Retreat reads, on the front, "We are...under construction." On the back there is a caution diamond and inside the diamond it says, "God at work." Under that is Zechariah 13:9, which reads, "This third I will bring into the fire. I will refine them like silver and test them like gold. They will call upon me and I will answer. I will say, 'they are my people' and they will say, 'The LORD is our God.'"

I thought about that verse that day out by the fire. I pictured myself in the fire. God didn't want me to lose my baby. Death took my child but God received him. I will repeat this truth over and over because in the haze of my grief it is hard to hold onto. Now that it has happened, though, God will use this experience to refine me, as the verse says—to draw me closer to Him. Things are a little smoky right now. I feel like my heart is on fire—and maybe it is. But I have faith that God will use it for my good and, greater still, for His glory. This doesn't mean, however, that the process will be a pleasant one.

Looking back I can see that He was not going to let me forget that. In the middle of the miscarriage, and then again the day after, God was right there, all up in my face. He didn't have any stupid, corny cheesy gooey lines for me, but He was present and persistent. Even though I couldn't crack a Bible for the three weeks following the tragedy, God found a way to reach me with His Word, regardless. His words, no matter how unnerving, were really there to remind me of the reality of His majesty; He was there with me in the middle of my tragedy. "I'm here. Sam. I'm not going anywhere. You can't get rid of me. I'm too big. I'm here and you're stuck with me, and, by the way, I love you."

You may not believe in God, or, if you do, you may not believe that it is possible to have a relationship like this with Him. He's real. You can't believe it just because I am telling you so, but I'm telling you that He's real. My honest prayer for you as you read this is that you know God's presence—that you will feel His strong arms holding you together and that in the stillness, when you are endowed with the peace that passes all understanding, you will find the courage to keep on living.

Listen carefully. If God is distant from your heart and from your life, it is not because He wants to be. In our crazy chaotic world it is so much more reassuring to believe sometimes that we are in control. It is much easier to keep God in a box than to unleash Him in our world. Maybe sometimes it would be easier because if our God was in a box, then we'd never have to change. We would never have to grow up and never have to step out in freaky faith to believe in the absurd notion of the resurrection of the dead. Plus, I've already told you about the "understanding" that God and I have. The guy is nuts. Maybe it would be safer to try to keep Him in a box. But then again, in one of the hardest, darkest, most painful, terrible nights that I will ever experience, I am so grateful that my Giant God was unleashed.

Big Giants Small Spaces

October 29, 2008

Big giants shouldn't sit in small places
Because they step on women's hats and men's faces
They mean to do well but because they're quite large
Their big fingers get stuck in tight spaces.

Big giants shouldn't stand in small places
With one stride they beat all at the races
Shy girls sly away from their hideous grins
And mischievous boys swing on their shoe laces.

Big giants shouldn't run small places
Small minds have no room and no praises
So take out your giant and let him roam
And the world will upturn by his graces.

As Misty said yesterday, after I broke down on her, "Sam, He's jealous for you. He's fighting for you." Unleashing God in your life is a *scary* thing. However, for the sake of your soul's peace, I would strongly consider it. Try it. In Revelation 3:20 Jesus says, "Behold, I stand at the door and knock. If anyone hears my voice [she] should open the door and I will come in and eat with [her]." Open the door a crack. I dare you. Test me in this. Make a little elbow room for Jesus. Let the light of the world shine in your darkness. He is your warrior-friend, your greatest ally, and He *doesn't* want you to be fighting this battle alone. He loves you too fiercely. I cannot even imagine how I would have faced the initial aftermath without Him. He is my umbilical cord.

The day after the miscarriage gave the No Good Very Bad Most Terrible Day a run for its money. I forced myself to leave the house for a few hours and I sat on Lori's couch, attached to her heating pad as if it were my lifeline and tried to explain what had happened. "Then this huge glob," I motioned with my hands.

"Liver," she finished. "That's what it reminded me of."

"Yeah," I agreed. We talked in her Living Room about other things for nearly two hours. That has seemed to help me the most. I talk about what happened with the people I want to talk about it with and only when I want to talk about it. Most people, however, have been really good about diverting my attention and, with Lori, we are such good friends that we were not hard-pressed for conversation topics. One of her favorites that day was how her washing machine had broken down with two football players in the house. As mundane (and slightly comical) as that may sound, it was like breathing in fresh air.

After a little over a week had gone by I went to visit with Lona. Her twins would be twenty-three this year. She cried as we spoke and admitted to me that I was the first one to ever ask questions in *twenty-three years!* I was the first one who had tried to understand what she had gone through. I was shocked.

The generation ahead of me gives my generation such a hard time for virtual communication. They say that we have forgotten how to talk face-to-face, but as I have talked to baby boomers, many of them shared a commonality. Many of them never really talked about what happened at all. Because it was a social taboo topic, most of them felt pressured to suffer in silence. Share your story. I don't think I can say this enough. You will release your hurt and you may actually help a friend in the process.

As Lona and I exchanged tissues, I asked her the question, "What did you need to hear at that time?"

"Nothing!" she said emphatically. "I didn't want to hear any of the sorry, gushy yaza yaza stuff." She scored a point for making me laugh.

"Can I quote you on that?" So now I have.

The bottom line is there are no magical words that can cure what was broken and there is nothing that anyone can say to make it better or take away the pain or bring our babies back to us. The only words that have seemed to come close are, "I know what you're going through," that is, by people who actually do know what I'm going through.

Or, as Lona's husband, David, said, "Been there and done that." He didn't mean it insensitively and I didn't come close to taking it that way. We were in church the Sunday after it happened and I broke down thanks to the lyrics of one of the hymns. It was hard enough to be surrounded by more than one hundred people and to be in the place where it had all started the week before. To make matters worse, I, perhaps out of paranoia, felt as if the entire congregation had me in their peripheral sight. In hindsight, it really would not have mattered if there had been only one heart trigger or fifty. Holding myself together was a futile wish that Sunday.

Farmer David handed me a handkerchief from his flannel breast pocket, a heroic act in and of itself. Any other day I would have given him a hard time for even having a handkerchief—who does that anymore—but as I smeared black mascara tears and lipstick all over it, I was grateful for the man beside me and the handkerchief. I quietly choked out the reason for my cry and David, standing beside me, spoke the best words possible in a way that only David can. "Been there and done that." There was someone standing right beside me who could not fix the pain inside of me, but who at least understood it.

I mentioned to Lona that I had finally stopped bleeding. "I distinctly remember wiping myself after going to the bathroom and practically cheering..."

"Because there was no more blood." (It quickly became a trend, as I talked to miscarried mother friends, for us to finish one another's sentences.)

That's one thing that you definitely don't really hear about until you've had a miscarriage. After a miscarriage bleeding and cramps continue for at least a week. Not only do you feel the pain and loss emotionally from losing the child, there is also a constant physical reminder, the devil in your ear saying, "Nanner nanner boo boo, you're not pregnant anymore. Ha ha." I kept saying to people, "At least if I was going through this pain for a child that is still alive I would feel like it was worth it." This statement, of course, would immediately throw me into tears.

Have you played the blame game yet? It wasn't your fault. You know that, right? It wasn't your fault. Your doctor better have told you that there was nothing you could have done. There is nothing doctors can do to prevent a miscarriage from happening or stop it once it starts. Don't wonder if they could have fixed it if only you had gotten to the hospital right away. One thing my grandma said to me between other random conversations was, "Accept that there might have been something wrong with the baby." Not only has my grandma had two miscarriages, she also had a son named Edward John who only lived until he was six months old.

My grandparents were married December 29, 1944. Two weeks later my grandpa left for Germany to fight in WWII. Grandpa and Grandma must have made impressively fast work of things because Edward John was born September 28, 1945. He died in March of 1946 of heart complications, just before my grandpa came home. Grandpa was never able to meet his first son. Their pain is much like ours.

About her baby's life Grandma said, "He was in bad shape. He would have had a hard life." She said the whole time he was alive he was crying and in pain. "In a lot of ways it was a hopeless outlook. Just had to trust the Lord and keep going." Her optimism was helpful. "[Now your baby] won't have to suffer through the ways of this wicked world, and you'll see him again one day."

Maybe, in the miscarriage, God was protecting us from complications beyond our wildest dreams. I don't know. I do know, though, that the miscarriage was not your fault and as much as you can tell yourself that in your head, receiving the message in your heart is a different story. The infamous eighteen-inch journey—the longest distance on earth. I keep reminding myself over and over and I will keep telling you—it wasn't your fault.

Your friends will tell you this too. Believe them, because they're right. That was the first thing Lori asked me when she saw me that Monday. "Are you blaming yourself?"

"I'm trying not to."

"Good. Because it wasn't your fault."

There is nothing that you could have done. If you doubt that at any point, just ask someone who you know will give you the answer you need to hear, like another miscarried mom. I did that with several of my friends. Their words were so reassuring.

Sandie said to me, "Sam, it wasn't your fault. They have their own romper room in there. There was nothing you could have done."

"Dia, did I do something wrong?"

"No, Sam, it wasn't your fault."

"Am I going to be able to have babies?"

"Of course! You're going to be just fine."

Anxiety. Another sentence in itself. As if worrying that it was your fault isn't stressful enough as it is, there are so many more insecurities that come with a miscarriage.

Sam: "I lifted that heavy box…"

Jenny: "Is God punishing me?" "If you love me so much, how can you let me hurt like this?"

Aunt Mary Beth: "God, Why?"

Dia: "Maybe I'm not able to have more children. Maybe there's something wrong with me."

Sam: "I'm never going to have children!"

Aunt Diane: "Maybe I did this. What did I do wrong?"

Misty: "Women are designed to have children. I can't even do *this* right!"

Lona: "Why did you tease me like that?"

You aren't alone in your fears or your uncertainties. All of these insecurities and questions are normal. Broken hearts can't be mended with the snap of a finger.

Like I said, the first time I broke down and cried was in the middle of church. Two weeks later I could tell I was holding it in. First thing in the morning, I woke up to the phone ringing. It was the doctor's office calling to tell me that the results were back from my blood work and the numbers were going…down. After a pregnancy that is exactly what hormones are supposed to do. However, I had hoped/ wished/ prayed that the doctor would say, "Shame on you, Mrs. Evans for having unprotected sex with your husband. You were supposed to wait six weeks to try again but it looks like your hormones are on the rise again. Your due date will be…" Nope. Instead the stupid nurse calls me *first thing* to tell me that I wasn't pregnant. I have to forgive her, though, because she had absolutely no idea what was going through my mind.

My husband came home one night the previous week and said, "So when do we get to have sex again?"

"Tonight works," I said. So we did. Then, the next morning I started *counting*. You know what I'm talking about: counting the little boxes of the calendar on the wall. And then I said to myself, "Hmm, maybe we shouldn't have had sex last night." I know that technically sex is supposed to be "protected" until after the woman gets her first period, but my husband and I couldn't justify "safe-sex" with a spouse; we've always had a little trouble with it. I wonder if he has the same Bible story in the back of his mind that I do (Genesis 38—the first record of a man ever "pulling out" that I know of). Read it and you'll understand our thought process. Also, *during* sex, yeah, not the best time to talk about protection. I'm sure I'm mumbled something about God's will be done but a more accurate translation would have been, "the hell with it."

After that my body had been doing some weird things for a few days. I had mild cramping and sore nipples. Combine that with the strong desire to be pregnant and with sex at a pivotal time during the cycle and a woman could possibly convince herself that she was pregnant—the way I did. And for four days that hope carried me—until the nurse called.

It turns out that the symptoms of pregnancy and the symptoms of PMS are very much the same. Let's talk about the first period post miscarriage for a second because most of us will get them (at least the ones who listen to their doctors). The emotional roller coaster of the first trimester is crazy-nuts. Clint would actually put his hands in front of him, move his torso simultaneously back and forth and up and down and say, "Weeeeeeee." Emotions after a pregnancy are just as bad.

We aren't supposed to be getting our periods. We're supposed to be pregnant. It is another physical and painful reminder that we aren't pregnant anymore. That first period (and many subsequently thereafter) will hit you harder than you wish they would. It's not just a cycle anymore. It's a non-pregnancy. You may just end up becoming an emotional zombie for the day. Misty was devastated every time she got her period. "I've never felt so much emptiness in my entire life—ever."

After the nurse called on Monday, all day long my body felt heavy. My chest was tingling with a slight sting as I held back the tears. I put on my brave face because the world refused to slow down for me. Despite my strongest hopes and teenage-like ignorance, the world truly does not revolve around me. The sky was a miserable shade of gray, which, in Oregon, is basically just a given, but it was a *really* hard day. The pain hasn't gone away as fast as I wish it would. It blindsided me on a day when I did not expect it. I was doing fine.

You'll feel so fine that you won't even realize that you are fine. The miscarriage, and the loss, are the furthest thing from your thought process and then *Bam Drop 'Em,* you're down for the count. See, lucky us, we get to experience all the side effects of post-pregnancy minus the child. The bleeding, the hormones, the weight gain and the pain. It's a really cruel trick, if you ask me, which you didn't.

Therefore, don't feel bad if you're a little *emotional.* Don't feel like you're supposed to be happy and perky and completely put together. Anyone that expects this of you is an idiot. Even my husband can tell you that.

Everything inside you is going to want to shut down. You'll wish that you had the type of depression wherein you *didn't* eat and, though you may have lost weight with the miscarriage, you may quickly add on even more pounds in fast food and couchpotatoitis. You aren't going to feel like listening to me on this, but I care about you and I want you to be okay. You need to fight for your health.

When everything in you is perfectly satisfied to stay inside the house for forty-eight hours straight, you have to fight the urge to do nothing and get up and do something. It is at this point that my dad's brilliant words come back to haunt me. When we were young, my sisters and I would be glued to the TV screen and it drove him absolutely insane. He'd come in and jokingly yell, "Do something, even if it's wrong!" Now I'm telling you…do something, even if it's wrong. Seriously, you have to move. Don't feel guilty at all on your sluggish days, but really try your best to get out of the house.

Eat lots of chocolate, by all means. Go to your favorite fast food restaurant and order "the usual" and, again, do it without guilt. Indulge yourself, but at a certain point cut yourself off and force yourself to be healthy. Go to bed earlier if you feel like it. Get your cardio on. Go for a run or a swim. The endorphins that kick in after a hard workout are a natural warrior against depression, not to mention that we can take our anger out on each stride and burn off those Burger King fries. Cry often. Crying releases those same endorphins. I always feel so much more at peace after a good cry.

Oh, and if you're watching TV or movies I would stick to game shows and cartoons for awhile. *The Price is Right, Cash Cab* and *Who Wants to Be a Millionaire* are always safe distractions, and the Teenage Mutant Ninja Turtles never had any babies. It would be just your luck that in the one episode you choose to watch, Michelangelo shows up with a "little dude." This is my way of saying, be careful what you surround yourself with. One of my friends is four months along and her Facebook picture is the ultrasound. Our friends shouldn't feel like they have to hide these things from us, but that doesn't mean that we have to unnecessarily surround ourselves with those things, either.

For many of the women that I have talked to, like me, their miscarriage was with their first child. For some of my friends, though, they already had children. As Dia said, "I couldn't 'cope' really. I had kids to take care of." Jenny, Lona and Monica expressed similar sentiments.

If you were already a mom, it is that much more important for you to stay healthy. You need to stay healthy for the sake of your loved ones. The healthier you eat and the more you work out the better you'll feel. There is always a storm before the calm. Even though white-knuckling it through life is no way to live, sometimes it's necessary to survive. It's like Hurricane Katrina just swept through and laid to waste everything you'd been building toward. Don't worry. Take a deep breath. We'll pick up the pieces together. The clouds are parting and the Son is fighting through. The calm is on its way.

Our Umbilical Cord

Small Steps of Faith

Monday and Tuesday, the first two days after the miscarriage, I was very much attached to a heating pad, as if it was my umbilical cord, my lifeline. It made me think, *What is my lifeline?* In between back-to-back episodes of *Dragonball Z*, I had time to think about the answer. The Sunday school answer is *"Jesus!"* which must also be said in the mocked, high-pitched gleeful sigh of a little girl. Try it again, *"Jesus!"*

The thing about Sunday school answers is that, while they are made fun of for being obvious, corny and surface-level answers, they are most often the *right* answers.

Who is our lifeline? *Jesus!* The Word of God. "In the beginning God created the heavens and the earth" Genesis 1:1. "I am the Alpha and the Omega, the Beginning and the End" (Revelation 22:13). Don't you see? God is book ends. He was there in the beginning, He *created* it in the beginning, and He will be there the day it ends. The second chapter of Genesis describes God giving Adam life by *breathing* into his nostrils. "God created my inmost being. He knit me together in my mother's womb" (Psalm 139). The Creator of the universe, of the sun and the moon and the stars and the galaxies, the same God who created waves that crash on the shore and trees that blaze with colors in the fall and mountains that point to the heavens…this same God created you and me.

He was there with us in the delivery room the day that we were born. When we learned to laugh, to speak, to walk and to run, He was there. He was there with us when we were gangly, geeky, self-conscious junior high girls. He was there through our first boyfriends, our first break-ups, our first broken hearts. He's been there, too, for all the bad things that we've done, those things that not many people know about, if any. And see, that's a good thing, because the Creator of the Universe knows all the worst things about us and still loves us to pieces and still just wants to be near us. I heard this quote once and it's kinda stuck with me. "If God had a refrigerator, your picture would be on it. If God had a wallet, your photo would be in it." He loves us.

God is here now, too, in the middle of this pain with you, right now as you read this sentence. Take a deep breath. (In case you haven't noticed, I am a huge fan of deep breaths. What can I say? They help.) Take a deep breath and realize that God is beside you in this moment.

Forgive my illustration. My mom and both of my sisters are phenomenal artists. My sister Jorie actually designed the cover and drew the picture based on a *text* I sent her. *I* can draw a pretty mean stick camel or perhaps a stick sheep, if you prefer? This picture, of the girl in the hand, is a sketch from one of my college journals. It's supposed to be me and it's supposed to be God's hand, but you'll just have to use your imagination because neither looks like either.

I came across this drawing after the miscarriage and the ironic parallels of what I had held in my hand (in fetal position) took my breath away. God was holding me as I was holding my child. God is still holding me. God is also now holding my child

While in college, I had one particularly tough night. I remember how and where I fell asleep. As for what I was actually upset about, I have absolutely no recollection. There was most likely a guy involved…

My bed was lofted and I, like any good college student, kept my clean clothes on the floor in a separate pile from my dirty clothes. This night I was so exhausted and emotionally drained that I didn't have the energy or the desire to crawl up into bed. Instead, I curled into fetal position on top of my clothes and cried myself to sleep. As I fell asleep, I pictured myself in the palm of God's hand. I was safe and protected and loved. That image brought me so much peace and comfort and that night I slept like a baby. I sketched my "drawing" shortly thereafter.

God is with you right now. He loves you passionately, relentlessly. No matter how far you try to run or where you try to hide, you will never be beyond His grasp or beyond His sights.

He is the hero that your heart is crying for. He is the soldier standing beside you to keep you safe. He is the friend, the constant; He has loved you all along and will never leave your side. When your world is falling apart, He will be the Rock upon which you stand.

Some of you may be really stinkin' angry with Him right now. I'm angry, too, really angry that He took my baby. I'm doing my best not to blame Him. I keep telling myself that God never wanted death. Death took my child away from me but God received him, *claimed and demanded* him on the other side. My head knows this but my heart will have none of it. My heart keeps screaming, "If you didn't cause it, then why didn't you stop it?! You could have stopped it from happening!" Then I yell, "Or if You knew that I wasn't supposed to get pregnant for a couple more months, why couldn't you have waited?" "Why would you, how could you give women such a beautiful gift and then take it away again?" The joking, politically correct, prevent-myself-from-crying way to say that to others is, "Man, I really want to box God right now, just throw down the gloves and go at it, you know?"

This is an open wound. I'm pretty sure that one of the biggest reasons God didn't protect me from my miscarriage is so that we could love on you together. When God gave me the title, I knew it was another one of our understandings. Each time I have sat down at the computer I have had to pray, "God, I don't want to think about this. I don't want to write about this. I'll do it anyway as long as You speak and I just type." So far I have not been able to make it through a day of typing without an accompaniment of tears. Deep breath.

I am writing this in the midst of my pain so that you will not be alone in yours. To be quite honest, I don't exactly feel like writing a book right now, especially a book about miscarriage— especially a book about *my* miscarriage. But here I am, because God and I have an understanding.

My friend Monica has a really unique way of looking at pregnancy and I think that I share her sentiments. "Sam, I'm just a vessel," she said, "God used my body to bring His kids into the world. They're His children." I think that I share her opinion in this because in every other aspect of my life God has had His way with me. But why not pregnancy? I'd never pictured giving God my pregnancies because I'd never been pregnant before. With seven children, Monica's had more practice.

We've all experienced tragedy and for most of us this isn't our first encounter with it. Following Christ doesn't mean instant success or instant wealth or instant get-what-you-want-when-you-want-to-get-it. Following Christ means that when we do fall, and when our world is falling apart, we can land on the solid Rock and we have a Savior who pulls us up again.

And, even if it weren't for God loving us through life's grimmest moments, God would still be God. He is worthy of all our blessing and all of our honor and all of our praise all of the time. Even when we experience tragedy in our own little universes and we don't feel like worshipping—God is still God and He still deserves all of our blessing and all of our honor and all of our praise—all of the time.

There are billions of people in this world that are hurting right now for a billion different reasons and God is sitting above it all, looking down and crying along with us. He is hurting because we are hurting but He is also hurting because even in the midst of our pain, in our stubbornness, we would still refuse to let Him heal our hearts when, in fact, He is the only one who can.

If God feels like He is a million miles away from you right now, it is only because you are the one keeping Him there. He wants to sustain you, breathe life into you, so he can give you His peace that passes all understanding. He wants to be your umbilical cord. He wants to let you fall asleep in the palm of His all-powerful hand.

The Soldiers Three
December 12, 2008

There is a man who walks beside me, our steps are trod in time
When I stumble in the dark his hand reaches out for mine.
Though nights seem cold and lonely I'll never lose my way
And when I am afraid, I hold on to that day.
That night so many years ago when I wandered from where I should
But then he came to rescue me and lead me through the wood.
I'll never forget the first sight of his smile or his eyes that beheld such grace
Though the world had waged war with him he didn't wear it on his face.

There is a man who walks before me that I should follow in his steps
He's walked this way, he knows my name, his light shines on the path.
Though we face great dangers his sword is always drawn
And though I'm not immune to hurt the battle wages on.
The trail we tarry is steep and rough but we must sojourn on
There are people lost in darkness hoping that we'll come.
They wear the burdens of their days and pile it on their backs
Their smiles have flattened with the weight of a world that cuts no slack.

There is a man who walks behind me, my rear guard and battle cry
He is my source of courage and the soldier in my eye.
The fearless man tilts his hilt to the enemies who hide
In the shadows of where we have been and the thorny roads that wind.
I will not surrender to the fearful thought of the demons that prowl around
Because I trust the fearless one whose sure steps shake the ground.

But I must never think that it is I who scares the cougar
I am simply a tiny cub with a mother on haunches behind her.
When life is hard and hope is gone and it seems that Satan's won
When darkness is thick and light is scarce and you're too weary to go on
Do not doubt the soldiers three who won't cease what they've begun
These three love you relentlessly, the Father, Spirit and Son.

Good Grief but Relief

"Umm, Sam, I don't know that I'm the best one to talk to about this because I wasn't sad." Monica admitted this to me while we were driving together one night. She was taking her two oldest children, Addy and Christian, to a drama class.

There were several reasons why Monica was not upset. Her overall outlook on life is "God's will be done." Beyond that, however, she was also raising six other children nine years of age and younger, had a feeling all throughout that pregnancy that she was going to miscarry and was battling depression.

Because Monica has given every aspect of her life to Christ, it is easier to accept her blessings from God as well as life's misfortunes. Monica distinctly remembers three years ago, while standing over the kitchen sink, God said to her, "You'll be tired for three years." She laughed as she spoke; we were the only two people left at Big Town Hero. "God *should* have said, 'exhausted and emotional.'" Throughout this whole disaster, I keep reminding myself that God will never give us more than we can handle. I think sometimes, as I believe happened in Monica's case, God will give us a little heads up if He knows that we will come red-zone close to our breaking point.

"Sam, are you ready to be blessed?"

"Monica, you're going to be tired for three years."

As God was and is with Monica and me, God is with you, too. Neither Monica nor I are extra special or super spiritual. She would tell you that as well. The only difference may be that while you might be keeping God at safe arms-length (the way I have been lately with the huggers), Monica and I have made room for Jesus to spend time with us in our daily lives.

"Sam, are you ready to be blessed?" He was giving me something to look forward to because He knew that I needed it. "Monica, [hang in there]. You're going to be tired [for a little bit]."

Like she said, God's "tired" was an understatement. Sydney is three years old right now and her depression cloud is finally starting to lift. Sydney is number five. When Monica was seven months pregnant with Sydney she broke her tailbone and was in so much pain that she could not carry any of her other children. When Sydney was ten months old Monica got pregnant with Cadence— and re-broke her tailbone. Monica said that because she was not able to work out with Cadence, that pregnancy was the hardest for her emotionally and the delivery was the hardest for her physically.

Cadence was three months old when Monica got pregnant again and she miscarried at six weeks (though nothing was discharged until thirteen weeks). Six weeks after her miscarriage she was pregnant with Eva, who is now nine months old.

When Monica said that she wasn't sad following her miscarriage, this was the story, the explanation that I waited for. The reality of Monica's situation is that her life was a whirlwind. She had four-then five-then six kids to look after while pregnant. Monica was on too much of an emotional overload to be sad. Her hormones were never quite settled before she was pregnant again. She was in a great deal of physical pain, too. "I don't know that I really could grieve because of the physical state I was in," she concluded.

That's Monica's story. Yours is different, but it's okay to not be sad. It's even okay if a large part of you breathed a sigh of relief. Remember, there are no rules for grief. If you happen to be happy that you aren't pregnant, as selfish of a reason you may think you have, don't you dare feel guilty.

Maybe you got pregnant with someone you never should have been with and you're grateful that you will not be connected to that person through your child. Maybe you're in high school or college and you have way too much too look forward to. Maybe you were raped and you see your miscarriage as a blessing. Maybe you have a supermodel figure and you didn't want to let that go. Maybe "other..."

I don't know your story; I just know that your heart has enough to deal with without suffering at the hands of your guilty conscience as well. Don't feel guilty. Your body has kicked into survival mode and it is going to cope and deal the best way that it knows how. Practice surviving. Practice living day-to-day. Focusing on life is a great way to give death good perspective and to put it in its place. "There is a time for every activity under heaven" (Ecclesiastes 3).

Some of you are not as sad as you think you ought to be and others of you are so sad it's hard to see clearly. If grief is a black hole, then I think depression is the inability to crawl out of it.

Did you know that the highest cause of stress/ depression/ grief is the loss of a loved one? Just because you never really got to meet your loved one, doesn't mean that he or she wasn't real, wasn't somehow really a loss. This is hard stuff.

Jenny admitted, "After four or five months it'd been awhile since I smiled and it would feel foreign to my face." Then she confessed, "I was barely making it through the day. I just wanted to die—I didn't want to die, but I wanted to cease to exist."

I feel like depression is a pack of wolves in the darkness that I am fighting off with a stick. But I'm still fighting. Are you? Are you being as honest with yourself as you need to be? If you are prone to depression and you are not finding your way out of your black hole, if you don't ever care whether or not you find the halogen exit sign, it may be time for you to call your doctor.

Needing a doctor doesn't make you crazy, not in the slightest. It makes you human. I asked Doctor Gwenn (a family friend and adult physician) what she would say to someone who was grieving. Her response was this: "It's really, really sad. It's important to recognize that it is the death of a loved one. Make sure you have people around you who can talk to you. If things seem to be getting more sad, then talk to someone. Lows are normal, but if you get stuck in a low then we have to help you get unstuck."

If you have to slow down, that's okay, but don't let your world come to a halt. Force yourself to keep moving. As Lona said, "Keep going. One foot in front of the other." Or, as Dory would say, "Just keep swimming, swimming, swimming." It's amazing how often her song encourages me to persevere. I shouldn't be surprised that Clint says I remind him of Dory.

There are things that I set in place to "Sam-proof" myself. "Make sure I…"

"I need help with…." Don't be afraid to ask for help. There are many people around you who want to help you but aren't sure how. Before and during my pregnancy I had been working out with my friend Barb. After the miscarriage I took three days off, but that was all.

Barb helped me stay in check with a daily workout routine and it was really helpful for multiple reasons. First of all, there is something very reassuring about the familiarity of a routine. It doesn't require much mental energy for me, but it keeps me moving. Endorphine kick—I've mentioned this more than once. Seriously, working out helps. It helps get your body back in good physical shape. I lost two pounds with the miscarriage. I added eight pounds in one week of depression weight. I have taken five off in one week simply by eating no fast food or things in the cookie-cupcake family and by exercising a few times. It also builds self-esteem and self-confidence.

Lastly, for now, when I am working out my mind unreels. It sorts, it processes, it unwinds. This morning Barb and I ran two miles in the rain and the whole time I was thinking to myself, *Bring it on, World. I can take it. You're not going to keep me down.* This thought immediately put Chumbawumba "Tubthumping" On a repeating track in my head: "I get knocked down, but I get up again, you ain't never gonna keep me down. I get knocked down, but I get up again, you ain't never gonna keep me down." It's a song about drinking, and certainly does not have the most edifying lyrics, but the chorus is a good mantra for you and me right now. Give your mind some freedom. Give it time to come to terms with everything that it has been through.

My questions were not all that creative the few days after. My mind was mush. Try having an argument with the all-time argument winner and the omniscient (all-knowing) God of the universe when on your *best* day, your wisdom is still His foolishness and on your worst day—well I might as well have had the brain capacity of a slug. I was riding my bike five days afterward and I felt like I was short-circuiting on Scripture passages.

"God, why?"

"The Lord gives and the Lord takes away" (Job 1:21).

"But why me?"

"God does not show favoritism" (Romans 2:11). He doesn't look at women and say, "Ooh, I like her more. She's never going to go through anything painful ever. And that girl there, hmm, she deserves a miscarriage. She's been naughty." God does not show favoritism and He is certainly not spiteful. So then I was left with my original question. The one that you have been asking yourself as well.

"God, why?"

"Brace yourself like a man. I will question you and you will answer Me. Where were you when I laid the foundations of the earth? Tell me if you understand. Who marked off its dimensions? Surely you know" (Job 38)! Through that I could hear Him saying, "The universe I created is much bigger than your tiny orbit. I know you're in pain. I know that you don't understand, but this world is bigger than you, Sam. Isn't it enough to know that the God of the universe has been by your side through it all and loves you and wants you to be okay? He's not going anywhere. Isn't that enough?"

At that moment it was.

Talk it out with God. No matter what you think you've got, He can take it. If you're relieved, if you're depressed, if you're pissed off, just be real with Him. He's super strong and super smart and He's had a lot of practice with this whole God thing. Besides, He already knows your heart better than anyone alive—even you. He created you with care and He cares about what's going on. He can help.

If you'd rather not appear to be talking to yourself as you drive down the road, or you're just more into that personal, tangible touch, then tell your friends how they can help.

God can watch the kids for a few hours—He's doing it all the time, anyway, but not in the sense that he could fix them lunch or help them go to the bathroom if they needed that. Ask your friends. That's what they're there for and they are dying to do anything to take some of your pain away, they just don't know what to do. Ask them. Can you watch my kids for a few hours? Will you go out to dinner with me? Can we watch a movie?

When I got home from Generation Life, a Bible study that I do with the teenagers, I was way more disappointed than I should have been that my Netflix'ed *Dragonball Z* was not waiting for me in the mailbox upon my arrival. There is something very appealing about zoning out and forgetting. There is something really tempting about staying there—especially if you are already prone to depression.

"Know Thyself." You know yourself better than anyone. Whether you are depressed or relieved, do your best to protect yourself from yourself. Find an accountability partner—someone who can ask you the questions that you know you need to be asked. (You may have to tell your newfound accountability partner what these questions are.) Have you showered today? Have you gotten fresh air? What have you done today to find peace or joy? When is the last time you worked out? When is the last time you opened your Bible? Do you need to get out of the house tonight? Do you feel guilty about any of this? Are you up for some company? When is the last time you ate a balanced meal?

Here are some hard ones: Have you told him yet? Have you talked to a psychiatrist yet? Is it time to go see one? Have you been taking your medication? Friends don't let friends stay depressed—now, if you'll excuse me, it's time for me to go. The mailman just arrived with my movie.

> *"October 7, 2009: Today I unlocked the door to my office and secretly wished that when I opened the door I would walk into a beautiful, magical place where I could forget everything and feel no pain. Much to my dismay, when I walked into my office it was simply that—my office. An overactive imagination can be a dangerous thing."*

Dear Daddy

Thursday, October 29, 2009 5:25 AM: God and I had another understanding this morning. It was useless to try to argue with Him. Two days ago my friend Penny and I were on the phone together, setting up a lunch date—so I thought. She was trying to cancel; however, she never got that far. She had a great practice run of it but the call had dropped. When she called me back she said, "Well, I tried to cancel but then the phone cut out. It was like God was saying, 'Nope! She's not listening to your BS.' CLICK." I'm glad I'm not the only one.

Sometimes God is the best listener in the world. You can vent, scream, cry, throw tantrums—and The Man doesn't budge. Other times, it is we who receive a swift kick in the rear when He cuts right through our BS and demands that we "pull ourselves up by our bootstraps," as good ol' professor J.E. Harvey Martin used to say. I once watched that short, scrawny eighty-year-old Canadian, Martin, check one of my friends into the wall all hockey-style in a race to get to class. True story. I digress. We're not surprised. This is Sam's brain at 5 AM. It's like that this-is-your-brain-on-drugs commercial. Anyway, now I'm up to write "Dear Daddy," because that was the understanding.

"Clint, I miss our baby," I said one morning.

"I know," he whispered, with a bear-like embrace and a kiss into my bed-head hair. "I miss him, too."

They don't have the same feelings or memories because the changes weren't happening to *their* bodies, but it was their child, too. Clint was excitedly on the phone with his parents and friends the day we found out. He was going to be *a dad!* People tried to warn us not to say too much to too many people, but a miscarriage was the furthest thing from our minds. We didn't understand why our friends and family wanted us to be so cautious. Neither of us ever dreamed that the statistic for miscarried pregnancies could be so high. No one ever talks about the pregnancies that *don't* work out—we only ever heard about the ones that do. So, in our minds, we were pregnant and nine months later we would have a baby in our house and neither of us could grasp or fathom an alternate reality.

"Clint! Clint!" he heard me calling from the bathroom. I was too shocked to manage any inflection as I beckoned him. He still didn't know anything was wrong. We suspected that it could be, it might be, but there was still no room for it in our thoughts.

For me, the scene change from soothing, relaxing bubble bath to Stephen King murder scene had been a somewhat gradual one. However, for Clint, as soon as he pulled back shower curtain number one, he was forced to take in the entire picture and the reality that accompanied it in one breath.

"Do you see it?" I asked, holding my open palm up to his eyes. I had to know that I wasn't crazy. My thoughts were so thick and hazy at that moment that I was unable, *incapable* of saying or doing anything to soften his blow.

"Yeah, I see it." But what he saw was gory and terrible and frightening. His wife was naked, vulnerable in a pool of blood, *her blood*, and our baby was dead. "Why don't you shower so I can take you to the ER," he said eventually. He was now standing over the bathtub, holding the shower curtain back. His mind had switched to autopilot. Now that the baby was gone it was his job to make sure that I was okay—that nothing would happen to me—that he wouldn't lose us both in the same night. His wife never sees things his way at the right time.

"Why would we go to the ER?" Going to the ER made *complete* sense to him; it made absolutely *no* sense to me. The baby was gone. There was nothing the doctors could do to fix it. Why waste the money? I was fine. I knew that I was fine. Clint didn't, and that was our point of disconnect that night. The water had diluted the blood and made it appear to him that I had lost significantly more blood than I actually had.

It didn't help when I eventually did stand up to shower and he only kept hearing the phrase, "more blood, more blood."

"Can I *please* take you to the ER?"

He must have thought I was insane. "*No. I'm fine.* Clint, my body is doing what it's supposed to be doing. It's cleaning itself out." The image that he had seen of me in the bathtub began to come into focus, though, until now, it hadn't really penetrated. "This blood is *extra* blood, the *baby's blood*, not mine. I'm okay. I'm okay," I tried to reassure him.

As I fell to pieces with the realization that I wasn't pregnant anymore, Clint was in the bathroom, sitting on the toilet, powerless to fix what was broken inside of me.

For Clint, the feeling of loss was overshadowed by helplessness. "I felt numb and powerless," he later told me. "I couldn't do anything to make it better or to make it go away." His child, his offspring, had died inside of me and there was nothing that he could do. To make matters worse, the death of the child was torturing his lover and the most he could do was stand by and watch it happen.

His mind was swarming. Had he not been gentle enough with me? Was there something that I carried that he should have insisted on lifting instead? He desperately searched for a way to shoulder the blame, to share ownership in the pain that I was experiencing. This became clear to me one morning when he said, "If our next pregnancy ends in a miscarriage as well, then I am going to go to the doctor to get myself checked out."

I tried to tell him that there was no possible way it was his fault but he couldn't hear me. More than anything, that tell-tale statement revealed to me how much he had wanted to carry the burden himself and was sick in his gut because he couldn't.

The morning after the miscarriage we went to the doctor's office together. At first I couldn't find him, after changing back into my clothes, when I was ready to go. Eventually I looked outside. I saw him but I didn't recognize him at first; I'd been looking for a strong, powerful, fearless man. But after a double-take I noticed that the crumpled man on the bench was my husband. He was hunched over. His shoulders were draped over his thighs, his head nearly between his knees. He sensed my presence and when he slow-motioned his upper torso to look up at me, tears were smeared all over his face.

I later asked Clint what the breaking point had been and he replied, "That guy in the lab. That's when it hit me—life's hard." As I was getting my blood drawn for my falling HCG levels, I asked the technician, Sam, about a picture that he had on his wall—a blue, purple and yellow chalk sketch of an angel. Sam explained that a few years back his daughter, Samantha, had died in a motorcycle accident. Someone had drawn that for him to remind him of his angel.

At that moment Clint felt the weight of loss, not just *our* loss, but the loss of a life loved that every human will experience, whether spouse or parent, child or friend, none of us escapes the misery and loneliness of watching a loved-one pass on. And his hurt, in addition to what his wife was going through, was too much to bear. Clint is my knight in shining armor. He would do anything if it meant making me happy or saving me from pain, but as he sat there folded in half on the bench, he realized that there are some tragedies that not even a hero can mend. Clint was overwhelmed with the sad truth of living in a broken world—no one escapes unscathed—and that's when his heart broke under the weight of helplessness in his inescapable reality.

A couple nights later he went to dinner with two guy friends of ours, Dana and Andrew. "What did you say?" I asked when he got back.

"We didn't talk about it."

"What do you *mean*?" As a woman this made no sense to me. I had been telling my friends all about it and they were graciously listening through details I'm sure they would have preferred never hearing. How could Clint get together with his friends for a miscarriage pick-me-up and not talk about the miscarriage? I was thoroughly confused.

"Well, they said they were sorry, but what else could they say? There was nothing to say. It just felt good to hang out with them. We talked about other things." Oh, ok. That answer made a little more sense to me.

But I still thought it would be healthy for Clint to talk it out, to come to terms with things. It worried me that he didn't seem to be coping as well as I was. He lost himself in the chaos of full-time school and schoolwork, allowing himself to be consumed by the effort necessary to attain a 4.0 semester. I suppose there are worse coping mechanisms that Clint could have reverted back to. Even though a handful of times I feared a relapse back into alcohol—no one would have blamed him—it never came. This tells me that he was coping better than I realized. But then, in that moment, that wasn't good enough for me. Yet, every time I mentioned the word "feelings" Clint would scowl at me as if I were using a dirty word.

I knew that there were more thoughts being held prisoner in that thick 7-7/8 skull of his, but he never wanted to *talk about it.* We women are so funny. We talk to cope, talk through our problems, but men internalize and process and ingest. When I try to get more than one word he looks at me this with this disgruntled caveman demeanor. *He* knows what he's thinking. Why should he have to share?

It made me angry that I couldn't get more than shrugs and grunts from the guy. I wanted to know what he was thinking. I'm starting to get that tense feeling in my heart just remembering how I felt, on the verge of pounding my fists on the floor in protest. So if he wouldn't answer me, then I would do the next best thing—talk about him behind his back. Now, in my defense, there was no premeditated assault. The opportunity did, however, present itself when Dia came to visit me one night and locked her keys in the car. So I took her home and she and Dana traded places; he came with me to get their vehicle and Dia stayed home so she could perform some necessary motherly duties.

"Did Clint ever say anything to you about the miscarriage?"

"Not a whole lot," at least I wasn't the only one. But Dana, the husband of a wife who'd had multiple miscarriages, seemed to be perfectly fine with "not a whole lot." Dana knew how Clint felt and was able to fill in the silent blanks with his own feelings. "He's just really angry," Dana explained.

Now, "he's just really angry," well that's a full sentence there folks, and as piddly as it seems, it was much more substantial than anything Clint had said. Progress had been had. I pushed my luck anyway—wouldn't be me if I didn't.

"Is that how you felt, too?"

"Of course!" I actually knew the answer because Dia had told me that Dana was angry. I was leading the witness.

"Why?"

"We had lost a child and there was nothing that I could do to stop it." Huh. That was the same impression I'd gotten from Clint—powerlessness. So maybe he wasn't holding as much back from me as I thought. It's just that, unlike women, instead of men giving answers to describe how they feel that are the length of a book—oh look, like the one I'm writing—their answers tend to be slightly shorter—like a word. Can't write a book with one word. But Clint's not trying to write a book. He's just trying to please his wife. So he sifts through his muddled brain glancing over frightening thoughts he knows better than to share with me, protecting me from the pain in his own psyche, and falls upon a safe word—powerlessness.

Maybe I should be proud of him for a four-syllable word, because even if he's not giving me the exact answer that I desire, I can never doubt that Clint loves me with every part of himself and that everything he does, he does with my best interest at the core of his heart. He would take on my pain in half a heartbeat if he could and I would never stand a fighting chance of resistance.

Be patient with your significant other, ladies. Don't worry about him if he's not dealing with it the way that you think he should be. He loves you. He's hurting, too. He'll come around. Maybe for now, that's all you need to know. That's all he wants you to know. That's all he knows how to say. He loves you. He's hurting, too. He'll come around.

If he is anything like Clint, then months from now you'll get one illuminating statement like a flash-paper fire—not a window to his soul, really, more like a chopping block. Knife up, see glimpse, the end. Clint's chopping block attempt at communication also came to me during a Sunday church service, while the pastor was preaching. I think maybe the pastor said something to trigger it, but at the time it felt like Clint was just blurting his *fe*li#gs* out at a moment when my attention was one hundred percent elsewhere to make the *shar@%g* as painless as possible.

"I'm a wounded dog." He paused for a second, extremely impressed by himself for the brilliance and accuracy of his own analogy. His eyes started to glimmer.

"Huh?" Clint's thought processes are just as erratic as my pregnancy mood swings. He can cover three completely different topics in the same paragraph and uses so many pronouns along the way that when I stop to clarify at the end, my interpretation is almost always incorrect. This time the double-take I did was worth it as I turned my attention from the pastor to Clint.

"That's *exactly* what I am," still proud of himself, not exactly talking to me.

"Huh?" My eyes were dull and dark as I waiting for the explanation that would also answer the question, "What the heck are you talking about?"

"I'm a wounded dog. You know, a wounded dog gets hurt and it needs help but someone gets too close and…" his sentence ran out of steam.

"And it'll bite him…huh," I finished. Huh, as in, "oh, that makes good sense."

"Aren't I good with analogies? I'm awesome at analogies. I like this pastor a lot. Like the way he preaches…" and he was gone. Chopping block down.

I smiled my pursed-lip, dimpled smile, simultaneously shaking my head and nodding as I tuned back into Pastor Warren Stroup's sermon about the Prodigal Son. I glanced at Clint through my peripheral. Wrinkled forehead, downward pointing eyebrows and tight lips, he studied the pastor's words as he spoke. "Huh. I didn't know that. Did you know that, Sam?" Servants weren't allowed to wear sandals and so sandals were a sign of freedom.

"No, I didn't."

"Well, it makes sense, though. It's hard to run away without shoes on."

I laughed through my nose. Clint was going to be just fine.

The Big ~~Butt~~ But What

"On Mother's Day at church all these kids would come up to me and give me flowers and say, 'You're my mother,' and I was like, 'Well, I don't mean to be rude, but no, I'm not, you know?'" Aunt Diane recalled with a soft bitterness.

I can't promise that everything will be okay for all of us. I will not. Two of the women I talked to—Aunt Diane and Sandie—both had three miscarriages and neither of them were able to carry their children full-term. But what then?

Growing up, all of my cousins and the kids at the church felt bad that Aunt Diane was never able to have children. We knew that she would have made a fantastic mom from the way that she spoiled us rotten. In many ways, part of her story is mine as well. Aunt Diane and I have lived quite a bit of life side-by-side.

Pool parties and sleepovers. She worked for Remax and every year we "got to" dress up for the parade and ride along with the float. Somewhere amidst our family there is a picture of my cousins and me dressed in clown costumes, sitting on top of a station wagon. I must hate clowns much more now than I did as a child.

She was my youth leader at church when I was in junior high and high school. Actually, even before I was old enough to go on youth outings I got to go because she was there. There was one retreat in my eighth grade year when I had a band competition the Saturday of the retreat. Uncle Brian (her husband) did nearly six hours of driving for me in one weekend so I wouldn't miss a thing.

I had a lot of medical problems (putting it lightly) as a child and I remember waking up in my hospital bed to Aunt Diane sitting beside me. In college I went into youth ministry and she became my mentor—excited to pass on to me books, wisdom and advice. On a birthday only a few years back, she brought me to get my first manicure, pedicure and facial. Even though I live two thousand miles away from my family now, she has still made it out to the west coast to see me. And, every time I hear Matthew 6:19-34 I think of her, because she is the only reason I have that passage memorized.

Why am I telling you all of this? Because it is possible that you and I might not be able to have children or more children, as the case may be. Understand that as I write this I am praying and hoping that I am not talking to myself.

Let's not kid ourselves. So many people have said, "Oh, don't worry. It'll happen." Sometimes I need to hear that. Most of the time, however, I look at them and wonder how they could come up with such an unfounded response so easily. The reality of it all, as you and I well know, is that these well-wishers have absolutely no clue whether or not their empty promises will come true. We may not get pregnant again and if we do, something may prevent our bodies from carrying the baby to full term. I say this with sadness to which black and white letters on a page will never do justice. We may not get the happy ending that we have dreamed of since we were children and taken for granted throughout our adult years.

But What Then?

Love. Love. Love. Love passionately. Love ferociously. Hold nothing back. I know it hurts. I know that it may never get easier to hear a child gleefully cry, "Mommy!" and truck it full-speed on a crash-course for Mamma as if there is nothing on earth that child wanted more at that moment. Mother's Day might always be the suckiest holiday ever and the pity glances will only make it worse.

BUT I can tell you from personal experience, that if you are an Aunt Diane, that is not such a bad thing at all. You see, I was among the gobs of children who would rush to her on Mother's Day each year to give her a carnation. And, while mothers only received one carnation per each of their children, there were a few Mother's Days in which my Aunt Diane received dozens. Though it may have pierced a tender place in her heart each time, all of these children meant it with the most love that a child can muster. Auntie Di meant (and still means) the world to us.

There is so much life, quality life, that I would not have experienced without Aunt Diane. She is truly a gift to me—and I am just one. There are so many others whose lives she touched because she had the time and the means to do so. And, I truly believe that she will be rewarded in heaven for her sacrifice. How much more by her three children who will be there to greet her when she arrives! She is a mom. We are moms. And we have a mother's heart and a mother's capacity to love—this is one thing that we have learned through this process.

So don't give up, please don't give up on loving. Even though right now your heart may feel shattered and leaky, God is going to mend it and fill it to overflowing if you let Him. Your love is a gift that you can give to others.

There are so many children who have lost their parents or been abandoned by them (I can't fathom it). If you were to adopt, you would each be a gift to one another. Monica never wanted to have children of her own (so much for that). She had always had a strong desire to adopt and help children in poor circumstances. This world is broken beyond our own universes and is in some desperate need of good lovin'.

For those of us who may never have children, there are even more women who were never able to get pregnant at all. I don't believe that that pain ever truly goes away. However, if we do not learn to love despite our loss we will shrivel up. We cannot die inside just because our children have. I know that life seems dreary and bleak—some days more than others. I know that sometimes you wonder how on earth you could ever move on.

The other day I had this daydream. I was sitting in a row boat, I on one end, Jesus on the other. Bright, sunny blue sky, no wind, waves glopping against the wooden walls of the small rowboat.

Everything was perfect until I looked on shore. The entire white-sandy beach was littered with mothers playing with their children—smiling and laughing—everywhere I looked. Their laughter carried across the water and it made me sad.

Jesus followed my gaze to the shore and then turned to look at me. "Sam, would you be okay if it was just you and me forever?"

I stared at him and nodded, "Yes…I guess, Lord." The eyes of Truth saw straight through to my heart and I changed my answer. "No. No, Lord, I wouldn't be."

Then Jesus put Clint in my boat. "Would this be enough," He asked. I shook my head, no. Whereas before the miscarriage my answer would have been "Yes," my heart had learned to love on a whole new level and I had more love to give than Clint would ever be able to handle. Already he says, "So much with the kisses, so *much* with the kisses."

No, my heart was bigger than that now. All of a sudden there was a downpour of teenagers whom I knew by name. Nick kind of tripped into the boat and landed face first in front of Jesus. Levi jumped in behind him with much more ease and gracefulness. Casi sat beside me…and all these other teens from the youth group piled in. When there was no more room in the boat, they kept on coming, sitting on each other's laps and falling onto the floor, some hanging off the side, others half-in and half out—but they were all there. Not one of them was somber or sullen. They came in laughing and giggling and their laughter was so *contagious*. I was filled with so much *joy*.

I looked at Jesus through the much-welcomed chaos and He smiled at me—this knowing, mischievous grin that had "I told you so," written all over it. It was as if He had taken my emptiness on as a personal challenge. Our gaze was broken by the sort of commotion that can only be caused by teenagers and in that instant the entire boat erupted in laughter.

Who has God put in your boat to make you smile? This world needs your love. It needs *you*. (Insert an old man dressed in stars and stripes, pointing an old, wrinkly finger at you.) You are valuable. You are counted. You are important.

If you ceased to exist, the way you may feel you could right now, there would be an entire shipload of people missing out on some quality life experiences. Grieve, by all means, keep to yourself for a couple weeks, eat all the fast food that you need to eat, but then recover. Don't wallow in pity—that's selfish. Plus, it has been literally proven (by Dr. Seuss and *How the Grinch Stole Christmas*) that serving others actually increases vitality and heart-growth. "And the Grinch's heart grew three sizes that day." Brilliant.

I realize that to you I am only words in a book and I cannot force you to do anything. But seriously, from one miscarried mother to another, get that big **BUTT** up off your couch and serve others. It will expand your universe and heal your soul. Trust me on this.

Hope Rewritten

Oh, Snap!

I didn't know what to write for hope. My heart has been very jaded as of late. While I was contemplating what to write, God reminded me of a moment I had back when I was a college student. It was December 23, 2001 and I was making the trek from the Twin Cities back to Chicago.

In December, Minnesota is white—and cold. My left window wiper stopped working so, with my arm reached out the window and wrapped around the car frame, in a freezing temperature, I was physically pulling and pushing the wiper up and down to clear away the fast-falling snow. Somewhere along the way one of my contacts popped out, which made visibility that much more challenging. I also remember that I was taking a route that wasn't so familiar to me so I was very focused on what little signage lined the road, meanwhile comparing those signs to little lines and numbers in my road atlas.

If you think that I am crazy and irresponsible you are probably right, but have you ever just been desperate to get home, so desperate that you really didn't care what state you arrived in? I hadn't seen my family in nearly a year and nothing was going to slow me down as I made my way to Sweet Home Chicago…until I hit a patch of black ice and spun into a fairly deep ditch.

I got out of the car, which was facing the non-existent oncoming traffic, and stared at the cell phone in my palm wondering who I should call. I was in the middle of nowhere and the middle of nowhere doesn't exactly get the best cell phone coverage. My car was in a bed of reeds. If I could have shaken an eight-ball it would have read, "Outlook not good."

The conversation went something like this:

"Who should I call?"

"How about me," God asked.

"Oh! You'll do." I got back in my car, tossed my cell phone on the passenger seat with the map, grabbed the steering wheel and said, "God, please help me get out of the ditch." The prayer was not exactly Oscar-award winning, but it never needs to be with God—only earnest.

I reversed just a few feet and then switched gears and slowly drove up onto the road. I remember thinking, "That was it, really?" It should not have been that simple. There were deep snow drifts in the ditch and the tops of cattails were poking out. What seemed like a hopeless situation for me was a snap-of-the-finger-fix for my Heavenly Father.

And so, as I pondered what to write about hope, God purposely used the same language as He had that day. "What about me?" And with one question He brought me back to a time in which the answer had been simple for Him.

Faith, Hope and Love

"And these three remain: faith, hope and love, but the greatest of these is love" (1 Corinthians 13:13). If you don't recognize this verse then you haven't been to too many weddings. In Christian circles 1 Corinthians 13 actually has a nickname: "The Love Chapter." While this verse is recognizable to many Christians, as well as people who aren't, I am not sure that most people who read it or use it ever really give it much thought. Have you ever asked yourself why love is greater than faith or hope? Have you ever stopped to think about what that means?

Love is the greatest because it is the only one of the three that exists on both sides of life. Hope and faith are not required in heaven. When we die, we will see our Savior face to face. We will not need to have *faith* that He exists or *hope* that He does because we will be looking right at Him.

On this side of life, though, the broken side, faith and hope are a precious commodity. If you have ever said, "There has to be something better than this life," then you have hoped and if you believe that the answer to that heart's desire is heaven, then you have faith. I really think that this world would be in much better shape if everyone had a little bit of both. The pain of this world seems so crushing at times that those without faith and hope will not survive it.

On Facebook, not too long ago, there was a survey passed around on one's chance of survival in case of a zombie attack. Forget zombies. Let's talk about your chance of survival in the case of a lost job or divorce, an awful break-up, surmounting medical bills, terminal illness or the death of a loved one—even a loved one not yet born. How on earth are we supposed to survive this crushing pain?

The answer is hope.

Hope Escaped

Not once, but twice in Biblical history there was a massacre of Hebrew baby boys. In Exodus 1-2, Pharaoh was intimidated by the number of Jewish men being born and gave a decree that all baby boys be killed. But Moses survived and then became Israel's hope. He led them out of slavery to Pharaoh and into freedom, possibly using some "How to Lead a Nation 101" skills that he learned from Pharaoh, himself.

The second massacre is in the New Testament. King Herod found out that there was a king born to the Jewish people and in a failed attempt to kill that one baby, he had all baby boys ages two years and under slaughtered. He was trying to kill Jesus, and consequently, our hope. As Peter said, "...*It was not with perishable things such as silver or gold that you were redeemed from the empty way of life ...but with the precious blood of Christ... your faith and hope are in God" (1 Peter 1:18, 21).*

Jeremiah, in speaking of the tragedy he witnessed himself, also prophesied about Herod's decreed massacre five hundred years prior to its happening. Jeremiah was a prophet during the Babylonian siege and captivity of Judah. Men and boys were dying in battle. Old men and women and children were dying in the streets from the sickness and starvation that the siege had caused. Jeremiah watched from a hill that overlooked Jerusalem as the temple of God was burned to the ground, the city of Jerusalem was destroyed and those who survived death were carted off into captivity. Jeremiah may never have had a miscarriage, mostly because that tends to be a woman thing, but Jeremiah did understand loss and the loss of children.

Brace yourself. *"This is what the LORD says: 'A voice is heard in Ramah, mourning and great weeping. Rachel weeping for her children and refusing to be comforted because her children are no more" (Jeremiah 31:15).* Matthew quoted this in his gospel when he recorded the first century A.D. parallel.

Imagine a point ten miles from where you are. That is the distance between Ramah and Bethlehem. Jeremiah says that the pain was so severe in Herod's day that the women could be heard wailing for ten miles! What darkness had fallen over the lives of those mothers! They had to have felt like there was no hope left...but they were wrong. Hope escaped. He fled to Egypt with his mother and father and would one day return to redeem what was lost.

God saw Rachel's pain realized when He gave His only, His firstborn Son to be our hope rewritten. It was the only way to save us, not from the pain that we experience in this life, but from the permanent death and penalty for our sin, hopeless separation from God. *"For God so loved the world that He gave His one and only son that whoever believes in Him shall not perish, but have everlasting life" (John 3:16).*

We have each experienced the loss of a child, but hope does not allow us to wallow in grief forever. Moses and his people escaped bondage. The Jerusalem that Jeremiah saw destroyed was eventually rebuilt. Jesus escaped death once by the hair of his chinny-chin-chin and the next time He and death had a face-to-face, Jesus defeated him once and for all by rising from the dead. Grief is normal, but eventually we must allow hope in the future to propel us forward.

This verse follows the description of Rachel's weeping for her children: *"This is what the LORD says: 'Restrain your voice from weeping and your eyes from tears, for your work will be rewarded' declares the LORD. 'They will return from the land of the enemy. So there is hope for your future,' declares the LORD. 'Your children will return to their own land.'" (Jer. 31:16-17).*

"Don't worry," Jeremiah assured the nation. "Don't cry. They will return from the land of the enemy. So there is hope for your future. Your children will return to their own land."

As I read this, the words of the writer of Hebrews echoed in my head. *"They were aliens and strangers on earth...the world was not worthy of them" (Hebrews 11).*

This world is not our home. We are living in enemy territory, Satan's playground. Look around you. That's why our world is in shambles. Drug addiction, divorce, disease, death, killings, shootings, rape, sickness, poverty, starvation, greed, hoarding, whoring, scandal, fraud... Are there good things, too? Sure there are. I'm not trying to be a joy-sucker, but let's be real for a second. No one can make it through this world without having a heart broken. This is not what God wanted "life" to be like. As Paul says, "Our citizenship is in heaven and we eagerly await our Savior from there, the Lord Jesus Christ" (Philippians 3:20). God has something so much better for us in store!

The lives we are living are dingy duplicates compared to what God has waiting for us in heaven. "Now we see but a poor reflection in a [dirty pot], then we shall see face to face, then we shall know fully, even as we are fully known." You know where that verse comes from? It's 1 Cor. 13:12. It's immediately followed by: "And these three remain: Faith hope and love, but the greatest of these is love."

Heaven, great, right? You're like, so we can look forward to *death*? Is that the best you've got? No, it's not. That does not mean that I have given up on finding joy in this life. We need to smile before then. Are you ready to be blessed now? Do you truly believe that God wants to bless you? Maybe? Not quite? You'll get there.

Here, you've heard this one before, right? It's always darkest before the dawn. Or how about this one, a little less well-known: Friday always comes before Sunday.

Friday, when Jesus was hanging on that dirty, splintered cross, He didn't look so glorious. Things didn't look too great for us either. Our hope died tacked to a tree. So much for Hope escaping. Jesus eluded all these near-death experiences, only to be killed like a criminal? He allowed those who wanted Him dead to catch up to Him the way an older sibling intentionally loses in a game of tag. To the world, it looked like Game Over.

But Jesus knew that Sunday came next and Hope didn't just *escape* death. Hope punched death in the mouth and defeated that sucker. And that man, named Hope, if He is strong enough to take on death and win, then He is certainly strong enough to hold you and I together today and always. God's blessing capacity cannot be measured. To say that He has no blessing capacity would be more accurate. This is my favorite prayer in the whole Bible...

"I ask you, therefore, not to be discouraged...For this reason I kneel before the Father from whom His whole family in heaven and on earth derives its name. I pray that out of His glorious riches He may strengthen you with power through His spirit in your inner being so that Christ may dwell in your hearts through faith. And I pray that you, being rooted and established in love, may have the power together with all the saints to grasp how wide and long and high and deep is the love of Christ and to know this love that surpasses knowledge—that you may be filled to the measure of the fullness of God. Now to Him, who is able to do immeasurably more than we could ever ask for or imagine, according to His power that us at work within us, to Him be the glory in the church and in Christ Jesus throughout all generations. Amen" (Ephesians 3:13-20).

Line Up Your Cross-Hairs and Let Go

On a gun, the sight is a tiny, little cross and, in order to shoot the target, one must be focused, looking at the target and nothing else. If all that you're focused on is the glum-dum-ho-hum side of life, that is all you will ever see in your crosshairs. Set your sights on the blessings of the Lord, who is worthy to be praised even when we don't feel like it.

I'll take my cue from Jeremiah. Babylon left nothing worth anything unscorched. Crops burned, livestock slaughtered—the people that gave the city life were all destroyed. In my opinion, Jeremiah was having a No Good Very Bad Most Terrible Day. This is Jeremiah focused on the pain.

"I am the man who has seen affliction by the rod of His wrath. He has driven me away and made me walk in darkness rather than light; indeed, He has turned His hand against me again and again, all day long. He has made my skin and my flesh grow old; and has broken my bones. He has made me dwell in darkness like those long dead. He has walled me in so I cannot escape; He has weighted me down with chains. Even when I call out or cry for help, He shuts out my prayer. He has barred my way with blocks of stone; He has made my paths crooked.

Like a bear lying in wait, like a lion in hiding, he dragged me from the path and mangled me and left me without help. He drew His bow and made me the target for His arrows. He pierced my heart with arrows from His quiver, I became the laughingstock of all my people; they mock me in song all day long. He has filled me with bitter herbs and sated me with gall. He has broken my teeth with gravel, He has trampled me in the dust. I have been deprived of peace; I have forgotten what prosperity is.

So I say, 'My splendor is gone and all that I had hoped from the LORD. I remember my affliction and my wandering, the bitterness and the gall. I well remember them, and my soul is downcast within me.'" (Lamentations 3:1-20).

Did God really pound Jeremiah's teeth in with gravel American History X style or make him the target of His arrows? No. Did Jeremiah know this? Yes. Was God mad at him for venting? Not at all. God's a big boy. He can handle it. Jeremiah had been preaching for thirty years to warn Israel that if they didn't turn their hearts back to God, God was going to remove His protection from them. They would have none of it.

Jeremiah must have felt like a failure, as he sat up on that hill watching a lifetime of loving effort going up in smoke. He was clearly angry with God and not afraid to show it. You and I may not understand his exact situation, but we understand his grief—the choking pain that feels like it will never go away. This is why I take my cue from Jeremiah in this—because despite everything he went through, even in the midst of his grief, Jeremiah kept his sights on the worthiness of God. This is Jeremiah focused on God's glory.

"Yet this I call to mind and therefore I have hope. Because of the LORD'S great love we are not consumed, for His compassions never fail. They are new every morning; great is Your faithfulness. I say to myself, 'The LORD is my portion; therefore I will wait for Him.' The LORD is good to those whose hope *is in Him; to the one who seeks Him; it is good to wait quietly for the salvation of the LORD. It is good for a woman to bear the yoke while she is young. Let her sit alone in silence for the LORD has laid it on her. Let her bury her face in the dust—there may yet be* hope.

…For men and women are not cast off by the LORD forever. Though He brings grief, He will show compassion, so great is His unfailing love. For He does not willingly bring affliction or grief to the children of men…

I called on Your Name, O LORD, from the depths of the pit. You heard my plea: 'Do not close Your ears to my cry for relief.' You came near when I called you and you said, 'Do not fear.' O LORD, you took up my case. You redeemed my life. You have seen, O LORD, the wrong done to me. Uphold my cause" (Lamentations 3:21-33, 55-59)!

Jeremiah began with a microscope on his grief. That is all that he saw, at first. He just vented to the LORD—illogical, unreasonable, inaccurate, loud, painful and *relieving*. Then he stopped and I believe, maybe, it was God who stopped him saying, "Child, look at me. I know you're hurting, but I love you." I can see Jeremiah realigning his sights on the LORD, and as he looked to God he saw the truth. "Yet," he said, "My God is faithful. He has a never-ending compassion. He is my hope and my portion."

And then, with eyes still fixed on our Heavenly Father, Jeremiah took a deep breath, maybe several. As he said, it is good to sit in silence and wait patiently for the LORD. It was in the silence and the long, deep breaths that God drew near to him. It was in the silence that God comforted his weeping and restored peace to his heart. As the pain subsided, for the moment (it would flare up again and God would pull Jeremiah through the same process once more), Jeremiah acknowledged that God had heard his cry and seen his pain. Then, when his perspective was in tact, Jeremiah boldly asked the LORD to uphold his cause.

Have you vented? Have you fixed your sights on the Majesty of God? Have you realized the endless possibilities of blessing that He wants to delight you with? Have you sat in silence and felt His presence at your side? Do you know that He loves you? Are you ready to ask Him to fight for you, to fulfill your hopes? He is standing by, waiting for your sight-aligned requests.

But remember, we can't receive the blessings that God is holding out to us if we are clenching with white knuckles *our* interpretations of God's blessing, of what we know we want and think we need in order to be happy. What is even sadder is that we often hold on to anger or sadness because it becomes comfortable and then we wonder why we're still so unhappy. We need to let go. Jeremiah didn't stay on that hill forever. Neither did Jesus. We need to let go.

When I heard the poem below, nearly twenty years ago, I nearly instantly had it committed to memory. It is the most beautiful, simplistic description of the tug-of-war that I am constantly having with God. Because, who said letting go, moving on was easy?

As children bring their broken toys, with tears, for us to mend,
I brought my broken dreams to God
Because He was my friend.
But then instead of leaving Him in peace to work alone,
I hung around and tried to help with ways that were my own.
At last I snatched them back and cried,
"How can You be so slow?!"
"My child," He said, "What could I do?
You never let them go."
~ Author Unknown

Silly Paul

The Sanhedrin were white-gloved sort-of folks. They had great power, authority and sway over all things ecclesiastical and political. They were revered. They were rich. They were respected and, in their opinion, they were always right. Jesus challenged their power and authority, was a threat to their wealth and spent a great deal of energy making them look like idiots.

Paul had been one of these snobs, appalled by those blasphemous teachings of Jesus and disgusted by the fools who had fallen for his lies. He says of himself: *"Circumcised on the eighth day of the people of Israel of the tribe of Benjamin, a Hebrew of Hebrews, in regard to the law, a Pharisee, as for zeal persecuting the church and as for legalistic righteousness, faultless." (Philippians 3:5,6).*

But then Paul had a very similar "understanding" with Jesus to my husband's—the 2X4 variety. (This gives me new insight to Paul's personality.) All of a sudden he found himself on the opposite side. The Holy Spirit unlocked him and he saw that Jesus was the law's hope fulfilled. *"Yet, whatever was my profit I now consider loss for the sake of Christ" (Philippians 3:7).* Flip!

See, when Paul was going around killing Christians, he thought he was just trying to snuff out a little candle wick. Oops. Silly Paul. Cuz' then he met Hope and Hope wasn't a helpless little candle. Hope was a light so bright that he instantly went blind. But it was only after he went blind that he was able to see the Truth (Acts 9). Leave it to God to form the perfect ironies.

Here's another one of God's favorite ironies. You'll like this one, she said sarcastically. Rejoice in suffering. Sounds like fun, huh? Paul, once he stopped persecuting Christians and became one, himself, began suffering for the sake of spreading the gospel. Paul believed so much in the reality of this hope that he was put on trial for it again and again. As with the massacre of the children in Bethlehem and Jesus' death on the cross, Paul being beaten nearly to death multiple times doesn't really sketch the most vivid picture of hope. However, if Paul hadn't gone to such great lengths to spread the Word, we may never have gotten the message.

Romans 5:2-5, which Paul wrote, says, *"Through [Christ] we have gained access by faith into this grace in which we now stand and we rejoice in the hope of the glory of God. Not only so, but we also rejoice in our sufferings, because we know that suffering produces perseverance; perseverance, character; and character, hope. And hope does not disappoint us because God has poured out His love into our hearts by the Holy Spirit, whom He has given us."*

Is hope easy to hold onto? Not necessarily. It takes practice. Someone who knows I have been going through a rough time encouraged me to cling to Jesus. My mind was filled with a picture of the sick woman who reaches out in faith for Jesus' cloak and is healed (Luke 8:42-44). Then my imagination took it one step further (it always does) and as Hope was walking away, I was clutching His cloak, holding on for dear life, as I bounced on the road behind Him. That's sorta how I feel right now. Hope is elusive, but we have to hold on.

Tour Jetés Are Dangerous

A tour jetè is a ballet move. It isn't really hard. You kick up your left leg, straight leg, pointed toe, and then, while that leg is in the air, you kick the right one up as well. While the right leg is the air, you turn 180 degrees to the left and land on your left foot. The higher and swifter the kicks, the more impressive the tour jetés. It's harder to explain than it is to execute. I know you're tempted to get off the couch and try it, but before you do so, you should really hear me out.

Even though I had not been in rhythmic gymnastics since I was in seventh grade, for some reason I felt compelled to demonstrate, to my friends in college, a tour jetè. One of my roommates in college was in ballet, so that's probably where it came from.

Anyway, up went my left foot, up went my right foot, with impressive height I spun around…and then my feet, my thighs, my chest, my chin, my arms and my hands all landed at exactly the same time. Total pancake…and from such an *impressive height*.

That's what the miscarriage feels like to me, like it took my legs totally out from underneath me with impressive force. Ephesians 6 describes the armor of God, but there was always one piece of that passage that I didn't understand as well as the rest—until I lost my footing. *"Therefore put on the full armor of God so that when the day of evil comes, you may be able to stand your ground, after you have done everything, to stand...with your feet fitted with the readiness that comes from the gospel of peace" (Ephesians 6:13-14).*

"Ready feet" I've always understood. I picture football players doing quick-feet drills or boxers who never stop moving, are always shuffling, prancing, ready to pounce. But here's what finally occurred to me yesterday. In two verses, Paul mentions feet three times and the goal at the end of the fight—standing, just standing.

Sometimes, even when you think you're doing your best and fighting like a champion, even then, you may still get knocked off your feet from time to time. Heroes are the ones who get back up again. And after you've fought the battle of your life, your goal is not to run a marathon. The goal at the end of the fight is only to remain standing—with feet fitted in the readiness that comes from the gospel of peace.

The Peace That Passes Understanding

All throughout the Old Testament, especially Job and Psalms, surrounding passages that speak of hope, are the repetitive images of God as our shield, our refuge, our strength and our fortress. These images put us in a protected place out of harm's way. We are the football and God is the running back. We are the damsel and God is the Hulk around us, shielding us with His own body, His own protection.

Then I came to Zechariah 9:12 and I paused at the idea of being a *prisoner* of hope. *"Return to your fortress, O prisoners of hope; even now I announce that I will restore twice as much to you."*

Don't just hide in God's fortress; chain yourself to Him. Don't let yourself escape the safe haven of His love. Be a prisoner of Hope. Let Hope hold you fast in His inescapable grip.

There is nothing right now that will make all the problems in this world magically disappear. And the nice thing regarding what Paul said about the armor of God is that he didn't say how quickly we have to get up again. Despite the amusing vision I have of bouncing along the path, behind Christ, that's not His style at all. Jesus stopped for that woman and didn't move until she was whole again, until her body had been healed by her faith and her heart had been restored by the gospel of peace. Then, when Jesus did move on to continue His kingdom business, there was an open invitation for the woman to follow.

Where are you? Are you in the crowd, wondering if you should step forward? Will you? Will you reach out in faith and let Jesus heal you? Will you follow Him, when all is said and done?

"And these three remain: faith, hope and love. But the greatest of these is love" (1 Cor. 13:13).

It is with *faith*, that I now approach the throne room of heaven and with *hope* that I beg to be redeemed and consoled, to find relief and peace. It is Love that leaves His throne to kneel beside me on the glassy floor and wrap His arms around my fragile body, quaking with pain. And we'll sit there together for as long as it takes, until I am ready to stand in the knowledge of the gospel of peace.

The LORD doesn't want tragedy to happen to us. As Jeremiah said, "He does not willingly bring affliction." Even though God doesn't want tragedy, I believe that when it happens He uses it to set our sights straight again. Hope that you will be comforted. Hope that you will be joyful again. Have Faith that it is the LORD who will bring you to this Hope.

Tuesday, October 6, 2009: On Sunday in church we sang, "We Will Dance." The chorus says, "We will dance on streets that are golden, the glorious Bride [the church] and the Great Son of Man [Jesus]." For the first time ever in my life when I pictured Jesus, waiting for me on the last day, there was someone waiting with Him. It was my child. And I know that that picture was from God."

"May the God of hope fill you with all joy and peace as you trust in Him, so that you may overflow with hope by the power of the Holy Spirit" (Paul, Romans 15:13).

From Some Mothers to Another

I feel like we've been having a conversation, kind of, except that I've been doing all the talking. Now it's your turn... and theirs. The quotes below are other women's responses to the question, "What would you say to a mother who has miscarried her child?" If you wish, in the space below, take time to journal for yourself. You may need more room than you have been given. Don't stop when you run out of lines, stop when your heart has been emptied. This book, this process, is for you. Take the time you need to heal your heart. Let go.

Have you vented?
"Grief has no timetable." ~Sam
"Everybody deals differently." ~Dia
"Let yourself be who you are." ~Jenny
"Even God can't change the past." ~Aunt Mary

_____

_____

_____

_____

_____

_____

Samantha Evans

"Life has changed. You were thinking all about the future and now it's not going to happen. Life has changed in a big way so if you forget to eat or you sit in your car in the driveway for awhile, that's okay. Some days are good and some days are bad and you'll never forget. But you can't just pretend it didn't happen. We don't like pain, but at least it assures us that we're alive." ~Aunt Mary

Have you fixed your sights on the Majesty of God?
"Your relationship with the Lord is what will carry you through. I'm praying for you." ~Grandma

_____

_____

_____

_____

_____

_____

_____

_____

_____

_____

_____

_____

_____

_____

_____

_____

_____

_____

_____

_____

_____

_____

_____

_____

_____

_____

_____

Have you realized the endless possibilities of blessing that He wants to delight you with?
"Disappointment is God's appointment." ~ Grandma

_____

_____

_____

_____

_____

_____

_____

_____

_____

_____

_____

_____

_____

_____

_____

_____

_____

_____

_____

_____

_____

_____

_____

_____

"We're on a path and God has a plan for us and that's hope." ~ Dr. Gwenn

Have you sat in silence and felt His presence at your side?
"I would try not to say much of anything at all." ~Monica
"I'm sorry." [Big Hug] "There's nothing you can say." ~Aunt Diane
"Really hard things happen to people that change who they are. It's a really personal journey." ~Jenny

"Be still and know that I am God. I will be exalted among the nations. I will be exalted in the earth."
Psalm 46:10

Take some quiet time to reflect on verses of Hope. Don't scurry through them.
Job 8:11-14; 11:13-20; 27:8-12, Psalms 16; 22:9-11, 31; 33:12-22; 40; 42; 46; 71, Proverbs 13:12, Jeremiah 17:7-8; 31:15-17, Lamentations 3:1-33, 48-51, 55-59, Zechariah 9:12, Acts 23:6, Romans 4:18; 5:2-5; 8:22-26; 12:12; 15:5-6, 13, 1 Corinthians 13:13; 15:16-20, 2 Corinthians 3:12-18, Galatians 5:5, Ephesians 1:18, I Thessalonians 4:13-14, 2 Thessalonians 2:16-17, Hebrews 6:19, 1 Peter 1:3-21, 3:14-16

Do you know that He loves you?
"I see it as God protecting the parent and the child." Monica
"I don't need to understand. I just need to hold your hand." ~An old hymn
"Breathe. God's there. He's got His arms around you. Just believe." ~Sandie

---

Are you ready to ask Him to fight for you, to fulfill your hopes?
"Trust God. Talk to Him." ~Dia
"What God brings you to, He will bring you through." ~Ruth
"Let the Lord help you because the Lord helped me." Grandma to
Jenny

Samantha Evans

He is standing by, waiting for your sight-aligned requests.
"I love you and I'm in your corner." ~Sandie

Living a Life of Purpose

How are you doing today? Today is a hard day for me—gray skies, heavy heart. I miss "normal." The night that I talked to Jenny she referenced what Don Piper, author of *Ninety Minutes in Heaven,* refers to as "the new normal." Piper encourages his listeners to turn bitterness into betterness and disappointments into divine appointments. Jenny said that she never even dreamed miscarriage could happen to her—as if she were invincible. That sobering reality is a lot to deal with.

At moments it seems impossible to move on, but moving on is exactly what we need to work toward. We need to move toward our "new normal" because living in bitterness, pain and grief is not really living at all. It is the *opposite* of what Jesus meant when He said, "I have come that they may have life and have it to the full" (John 10:10).

I wish that I was better right now, but I'm not. There's no formula to follow to speed up the grief process. There is no way to hurry ourselves through it. Grief has no timetable. Our bodies and our hearts will heal as they see fit. For me, this is disappointing. I'm a take-action kind of gal. Something needs to be done, so okay, let's do it instead of sitting around and talking about it. Healing from tragedy doesn't work that way and that drives me crazy. Now, you know me a little by now. You know that Patience and I do not understand one another.

There was a song by Rappin' Rabbit that my sisters and I used to listen to as kids called "Patience." I've had that crazy children's song in my head for twenty years and I totally empathize with the cartoon bunny who sings, "I can't wait to have patience, because patience is a wonderful thing. Hurry up, let me have it. Gotta get it now; I want it more than anything. This has taken long enough. Give me some of that patience stuff. I can't wait to have patience. Hurry up. Hurry up. Hurry up!"

So Patience and I are a work in progress. I feel like other people wonder why I'm still struggling with this, but I'm pretty sure that's my own insecurity speaking, my own desire to *be* done with this already. A couple weeks ago a friend from church said, "I just want to see your smile again." I do too. Our friends may miss "us," the women that we used to be, but our friends will just have to wait. Even when we find our smiles again, we will never be the same.

Maybe you're better at patience. Maybe, for you, knowing that grief has no timetable takes off the pressure you've felt and allows you to breathe. *Whew! I'm* not *behind schedule? What a* relief! Let go of whatever preconceived notions you have about what you are supposed to be like right now, what duties you feel like you have to perform, pressures that you feel others are putting on you, and be okay with imperfection. We cannot stop moving altogether. The world is still turning. The sun will shine without our help.

One thing that should be clear to all of us now, though, is that life is a gift, a precious, precious gift. Each life also has a purpose. This may be hard for you to understand right now, but our babies all had a purpose on this earth as well. Look at mine—he (or she) gave me sympathy for something that I never could have understood otherwise. I've written a book, for goodness' sake. Your baby has had a purpose too.

Maybe your baby/ babies lived to realign your crosshairs.

Maybe you are supposed to share your story with someone else. Stop and think of all the women you had heard of miscarrying before you. What was your response when it happened? "Oh, that's too bad." [End thought.] That doesn't really quite cover it anymore, does it?

Did God teach you how to love? Misty gently said to me one day, "Not that you needed this lesson. You are truly a mom; you have a mother's heart. You know what sacrifice is—and unconditional love."

You thought about every food morsel that you put in your mouth in a whole new way. Every activity you participated in made you wonder if that was okay for your child. You and I cared for our children when they could give us absolutely nothing in return. Just them being there, inside of us, growing, safe and protected, that was enough.

And now, now that we've lost them, you and I feel real pain, raw, knock-the-wind-out-of-you, earth-shattering, uncut pain, but when the pain subsides, you are the only one who can see your child's purpose fulfilled. Your child has changed your life and you have a chance to live your life in a way that will honor your baby.

Your child was real. Our children were real. Don't feel silly for thinking that, even if others have trouble comprehending it. Our babies' lives were lives worthy of celebration—they still are. Celebrating your child's life in some way is part of the healing process. How have you remembered your child? Have you journaled the story? Drawn pictures? Had a memorial service? Next Sunday in church, on All Saints Day, we'll read of the names of members of our church who have passed away this last year. "Baby Evans" will be on that list. I've also thought about donating flowers to church the Sunday closest to the due date.

It doesn't have to be a huge ceremony—but it can be. Robert, whom my Aunt Mary had after her second miscarriage, turns eighteen this November, so it took her a moment to figure out the timing of it all. As she thought back to her second miscarriage, she said, "Well, the girls were old enough to put flowers on the casket." I held in a gasp. She'd had her child buried. Aunt Mary did what she needed to in order to honor her child's life and move on, knowing that she had done everything she could to love her baby. I would have been younger than ten years old at the time and I don't remember the ceremony; I don't remember whether or not I was there, but other family members do. My mom and dad remember it. So does my Aunt Diane. Remember your child.

Aunt Mary still misses her baby. "Every November, I'm sad," she told me. Aunt Mary may not have ever been able to exchange that first glance with her baby, but she understood that it was a real life. As we spoke she chuckled at a memory and then shared it with me. "One of my very good friends brought me balloons to celebrate that life," she remembered.

There are a ton of things that you can do—simple things. Plant a rosebush in honor of your child. Put that picture of the first pregnancy test in your wallet or on your fridge. Eat cake on your baby's birthday. (The sacrifices you'll make!) The biggest way in which you can honor your child, however, is to keep on living. Make the most of every moment and cherish life.

In Job 11 it says, "[Your] life will be brighter than the noonday sun." Every one of us has experienced a sunny day, even if we had to leave our own state to find one. I'm pretty sure that Job wasn't referring to the Oregon sun, which hibernates eight months out of the year. We associate sunny images with laughter and sparkling water and smiling friends. There is a reassured peace that comes from bright days—the feeling that anything is possible and the world is a beautiful place. You know what I'm talking about, don't you? That image that you have in your head and the feeling in your heart that accompanies it—that's hope.

Jesus, our hope fulfilled, our hope rewritten, said, "I am the light of the world" (John 9:5). Jesus is our sustenance. He doesn't supply things for us that satisfy us, He *is* what satisfies us. Psalm 119:105 says, "Thy Word [Word in the flesh (John 1:14)] is a lamp unto my feet and a light unto my path." Jesus shines light on the path before us. His voice calls us by name and leads us through the darkness. He walks beside us to make sure that we will be alright.

Jesus came because we were a mess. We were dumb, we were lost and we were misdirected. I suppose one could argue that not much has changed. Regardless, Jesus came to do two things. First, He came to realign our sights. "You need hope? You need life? I've got these things to give you. I AM these things and I am giving *myself* to you, my life for you." All we have to do is look to the cross, put the cross in our crosshairs. The result of looking to the cross is that it *becomes* our crosshairs.

The second thing that Jesus came to do, once our sights were realigned and fixed on the cross, was to point us to a dying world in need of a little TLC (tender love and care), in need of a lot of it, actually. As followers of Christ, we look through the cross and we see the world through Christ's eyes. We see the reasons for His broken heart. Jesus may have been God, but as a man His lifespan was only so long. The last thing He said to the disciples before He ascended to His throne as our King was, "Go! Get off your duff and tell people about me as quickly as possible!" This is Matthew 28:18-20 very loosely paraphrased.

For inasmuch as Jesus promised us that He would be our hope and our light, He also called us to be the same thing for others.

You are the light of the world. A city on a hill cannot be hidden. Neither do people light a lamp and then hide it under a bowl. Instead they put it on a stand, and it gives light to everyone in the house. In the same way, let your light shine before men that they may see your good deeds and praise your Father in heaven" (Matthew 5:14-16).

As much as I was resistant to use my experience for God's glory, though the front I put up lasted all of five hours (four and three quarters of which I was sleeping for), I knew even then, in the middle of my grief, that this love letter to you is what God was calling me to. Now He's calling you to the same thing—to be someone's love letter from God. God calls us to a life of putting our lives on the line for others—to tangibly love others the way Jesus would.

Yesterday I was watching a movie and I got a call from a friend who lost a lifelong friend in Afghanistan. The part of me that was not interested in a long conversation was quickly shushed by the reminder of all those who had listened to me throughout my grief, who had been Christ to me, my light and my sustenance, through my pain.

God calls us to this daily, to look through His cross to see the needs and the hurts of the people around us. Listen quickly, because if not, I guarantee that there is a huge 2X4 coming at you from behind. God has given each of us gifts to share with others. He has given us these gifts *in order* to share them with others. We have absolutely no business hiding our talents under a bowl or locking them up to keep them safe.

Do you sing? Do you write? Can you draw more than a stick camel? Are you good with numbers? Do you knit? Are you good at puzzle-solving or repairs? Can you listen? Do you have three dollars to buy a friend a coffee or a homeless man a hamburger? Do you have the guts to share your story—not just this story, but the story about how God has worked in and through you even when you were paying no attention to Him? That's the life that God has called you to. That is what it means to live a life of purpose.

Jesus lived a life of purpose. His purpose was to give His life for us. It wasn't enough for God to look in on our pain from heaven. He decided that the only way to truly love us was to come to earth and live among us.

As I close out the few remaining pages of this book, the end of the calendar year is quickly approaching. According to the church calendar we have just entered the season of Advent. Advent is the time of anticipation before Christ's birth. Are you ready? Is it time yet? These are Advent questions.

At the front of the church we have four candles—one for each week of advent—and each week we light another candle. There is a banner under each candle with words that encompass the season of Advent.

Peace, Joy, Hope and Love. These are good words, Amen? These are very good words. As I have reflected on them, the anticipation of the blessings that God has promised me has stayed close to my heart. God, is it time yet? I'm a young girl all over again, trapped in the back of my dad's minivan on a twenty-seven hour road trip to Florida from Chicago. Are we there yet? How about now?

At our first Advent service, Pastor Jeff asked me to read the gospel passage. When I opened to Luke 2:1-7, I saw, scribbled in the margin, the word, "Hope." Do you ever open your Bible, laugh out loud and think to yourself, "Alright, message received."?

"In those days Caesar Augustus issued a decree that a census should be taken of the entire Roman world...so Joseph also went up from the town of Nazareth in Galilee to Judea, to Bethlehem, the town of David...with

Mary, who was pledged to be married to him and was expecting a child. While they were there the time came for the baby to be born, and she gave birth to her firstborn, a son. She wrapped Him in clothes and placed Him in a manger because there was no room for them in the inn."

Advent—the season of anticipation of the Christ child, the season of hope. As I read the last part of the passage, I couldn't help but mischievously smile at the mirrored thought of the anticipation of a firstborn child. God fulfilled His promise of hope to humanity through Baby Jesus. He never asked me again, after that horrible night, if I was ready to be blessed. He must have known the answer was yes because He kept His end of the bargain.

A few weeks after the miscarriage happened I wondered if God really ever was going to give me my dream of having a child. Then I had this fear that maybe my dreams were not in alignment with what God wanted for me. Maybe He wouldn't give them to me because they weren't right for me. But that didn't fit. As I have reread my story I have realized that even as I have typed God has brought me beyond my grief. I started with a microscope on the pain of that day, my impatience for everyone around me and misconceptions about what in the world God was thinking up there.

Now here I am, ready to speak my sight-aligned requests, which are no secret to any of us…I didn't have to voice them at all because He beat me to them. Praise the Lord for being unleashed in my life and answering prayers with the sense of humor that only God can. *"There is no fear in love. But perfect love drives out fear"* (1 John 4:18a). Now I have faith that God gave me my dreams so that I could watch Him fulfill them.

Wait, is she saying? Yes, I am. Sam I am pregnant. I am both thrilled to tears and terrified.

Do you know; can you fathom how much He loves and how much He wants for you? You are His precious child and He is jealous for you. He wants to be your everything. The God of the Universe loves so you much that He just wants to be near you—and your dreams—He wants to give them to you. Have faith.

That's Not a Wrap

So, it turns out that I was pregnant again a few days after the nurse's phone call telling me that I wasn't pregnant. I was really excited about ending my story by telling you that I was pregnant, but that wasn't what the Author intended. He had a different plan—He always does. You'd think I'd get the hang of this by now. I think one thing and He does the other—I told you that in the beginning; this was the understanding that God and I had…and yet, His ways never cease to surprise me.

It made sense to me that I would get pregnant two weeks after the miscarriage—the cutsie story I would be able to tell of my blessing fulfilled—and yet, that I understood the plan should have been my first clue that it was not what God intended. I was so happy because I felt redeemed. Now I feel as if there is something wrong with me and I won't be able to chase away this demon until I can successfully carry a child to full term.

I thought that I was keeping it together pretty well but today I went to a funeral. That was my first mistake. The whole time, all I could think about was how I jealous I was of this woman who had passed on because she would get to meet my children before me. Then I had this Holy Spirit inconvenient reminder in the back of my mind… "Never your children to begin with." Surrendering, the word "no," these are things that I have never been really good at.

I had been more guarded throughout this pregnancy. Careful. Clint was finally beginning to acknowledge it. We got farther this time. The due date was within days of my father's birthday. It was a healthier pregnancy at first—I could feel it—and I had all the weight to go with it. I was already wearing maternity pants. I put away all the clothes that I knew would not be fitting me for a very long time. We were four days from our first ultrasound and I had visions of sending the pictures to family members in Christmas cards. I was counting down the days until I could text Debi again saying, "Um…gonna be a little bigger for your wedding." Clint and I were arranging our summer plans around the birth of our first child. And then I started spotting. The cramps came and wouldn't go away. Another child came out too soon. I guess impatience runs in the family.

There were clues that it was going to happen. When I was first pregnant, Ashley, our big fluffy bowling ball, would not crawl onto my stomach. I think she sensed something growing inside me. Then a few weeks back she crawled onto my tummy…I started crying and threw the cat off my lap. It was like she knew the truth before I did. It's okay if you think I'm crazy. You're not alone.

The evening that it happened, in the midst of my "prayers" I started singing, "I will praise you in this storm and I will lift my hands 'cuz You are who You are no matter where I am and every tear I cry, You hold in Your hands…" I stopped mid song and gasped and the words the Spirit inside me had mustered. I was about to encounter another storm.

Now, I say "prayers" because they weren't really the traditional image of kneeling quietly beside the bed with palms gently pressed together while whispering sweet nothings to God. I was really more just screaming, "Please, Jesus! Please, Jesus! Please, Jesus! Please, Jesus! Please, Jesus" over and over throughout the day, occasionally adding the coherent thought, "Please, You're the only one who can save this baby if there's something wrong with it!" I was short circuiting on Bible verses again—my suffering flesh waging war with the theologically trained and Scripture savvy

Bible geek that is locked inside my heart. This time though, I was calling in promises...

"Just say the word, Lord, and my servant will be healed, for I too, am a man of authority. I tell this man go and he goes..." (Luke 7:1-10).

I reminded Him of the persistent widow (Luke 18:1-8). The judge knows He can give her what she wants. The widow knows that He is her only hope.

"Even dogs get the crumbs that fall to the floor of their master's table" (Matthew 15:21-28).

I reminded Jesus of all the people He'd healed and all those He'd raised from the dead. I knew that it wasn't His fault, but I also knew that He had the power to stop the miscarriage from happening. I promised Him that I would give Him credit and glory for saving my child from the brink of death as if I'd be doing Him some sort of favor in return for letting me keep the baby.

Then I finally yelled out, "This was the blessing that you promised me!" The only clear words I heard from Him that night were, "No, Sam, it wasn't." And for obvious reasons I didn't hear those words at first, either. I didn't want to hear them.

I felt alone and wondered what I had done to cause Him to turn His face from me. Why hadn't he answered my prayers? Then yesterday I get this call at the church. It was Friday and I nearly did not pick up. Pastor and I have secret office hours when we happen to be at church polishing details on our days off. I can't speak for Pastor Jeff, but I know that I never feel compelled to answer the phone on these days because the office is closed anyway and no one knows that I am there.

I picked up the phone and answered a distress call from a frantic woman in our congregation who needed immediate prayer for her daughter. So I prayed with her over the phone. Hung up. Continued working. Five minutes later I get a text from her that says, "Wow! God is good." The impossible situation that we prayed through together—answered in five minutes. For the rest of the evening I went around with a dark Eeyore rain cloud hovering over my head. "Why her, God? Why her? You answer her prayer in five minutes but with me You remain silent." I was Peter, on the beach with Jesus (John 21).

I remember noting the time on the clock at 11:28 PM and sometime after that I realized that she was not the only one He had answered her prayer for. The request had come from my lips. The Lord was saying, "Sam, I still hear you. I'm still listening. Your prayers are still getting through."

Then I had yet another epiphany. This week has been full of them. Prayer will never work if I am praying, "My will be done." Faith that moves mountains is useless against mountains that God has not willed to move. Abba knows best—I trust that, even though I think the guy is insane.

Real life isn't like the chick flicks that I enjoy watching so much. The heroine always gets her way after one hundred and twenty-two minutes and whatever struggles she had to go through were worth it in the end because she got her happy ending.

We each cycle through times of happiness but the end credits never roll there. Time keeps clicking, constantly propelling us forward. Each of our lives is a never-ending story with future pages yet to be written. Our lives are choose-your-own-adventure books in which we don't get to backtrack when we don't get the outcome that we want.

In my quieter moments this last week I have reflected on the stories of Job and Hannah. Job lost his children and all of his wealth in the same day and then got an awful skin disease on top of that. Some things occurred to me with these stories that I want to share with you, things that, even if I have known them all along, carry a different meaning with them now in light of what I have been through.

First of all, God said to Satan, "Very well, then, everything he has is in your hands...he is in your hands; but you must spare his life" (Job 1:12, 2:6). Satan was saying to God, "Of course Job praises you. Of course he goes around saying, 'Wow, God is good.' You have given him everything he could ever want." But God had complete confidence in Job. Huh. He knew that even if he lost everything, Job would not curse God...and he didn't. The way that Job handled his loss was a testimony to everyone around him. The way we handle our losses will be a testimony as well. Job spends multiple chapters asking God *why* but he never says, "I hate the Lord. This is all His fault. He sucks and I never want to speak to Him again."

The second thing that occurred to me with the story of Job is that there is one person in the story who is there all along, connected to Job, who lives throughout the whole ordeal—Job's wife. It seemed an obvious answer to me…if Satan *really* wanted to hurt Job, to test him, he could have gone after Job's wife. But then again, maybe he couldn't. Maybe her life was linked to his by the "one flesh" principle. Maybe her losing her life *would have* caused Job to die of a broken heart and so she was off limits to Satan with God's command, "you must spare his life."

Never tempted beyond what we can bear—that's God's promise to us, right? He does know our limits, even better than we do. God loved Job and his wife. In the end, when God blesses Job with more than he ever could have asked for or imagined, Job's spouse is there to experience the blessings with him. Job did get his happy ending—just not the way that he expected.

And then there's Hannah. When I put myself in Hannah's shoes I realized that the prayer she prayed on the steps of the temple for a son was not the first time that she had prayed that prayer. In 1 Samuel 1 it says that they went to the temple "year after year." Hannah had been praying for children for a *long* time. God answered the prayer when it was perfect for His timing, and only after Hannah promised to give her son over to the Lord.

Her son Samuel was the transition between the judges and prophets of the Old Testament. Samuel anointed Saul as the first king of Israel and anointed David to be king Saul's place. He was one of the few people who knew David as a shepherd, a king and a warrior. Samuel's role in that pivotal part of history was crucial; God used him in specific places at specific times. In God's scope, Hannah's son was not born too soon or too late, but at the perfect moment to fulfill God's plan.

I have so many questions. Why me? What next? What happens now? Do I get to have children? What blessing was God referring to and when do I get to cash in the chips on this deal? Why did He let me get pregnant *twice* if the timing wasn't right yet?

But God is asking questions, too. Am I only your God when things are going well? When things are good? Is your love for me based on blessing? Do you trust me? Do you know that I love you? That I have not forgotten you? That I never will?

Has my faith been shaken by two miscarriages in three months? Shaken? Yes. Destroyed? No. God is still God. This has not dethroned Him. One of my friends said, "He knows you can handle it. He trusts you with more." Maybe she's right. Maybe that's why God and I have the understanding that we do.

I know this in my heart. "Are you ready to be blessed now?" That question has stayed with me. He knows what He is doing. I have to keep telling myself that.

It doesn't mean that things are always peachy-keen between the two of us. A few days back I mentioned to Him something along the lines that I wished He was human again so I could beat the crap out of Him. I'm pretty sure that this is not the way the Creator of the universe deserves to be talked to—but I don't think the comment really threw Him off guard, either. He has sole rights to my innermost thoughts…I have no secrets from Him; He knows all the feelings in my heart. Despite this fact, He still sticks around, which is a miracle in and of itself.

When I was a freshman in high school I went to Philadelphia. In a restaurant there, on the back of a sugar packet was the saying, "Friends are people who know all about you but like you anyway." And that's the best thing about God. I am a spoiled, selfish, sinful woman and He still cares to hear about what I have to say. When I pray, He takes my words into consideration. However, He *doesn't* let me act like a spoiled princess when I know better.

The following poem, if you can call it that, it's more a dialogue really, is something I wrote during my devotions one day. I was throwing a spiritual hissy fit and I could feel in my heart that God was saying enough is enough. As I vented I also imagined how God would respond.

Give Up or Throw Down
October 13, 2009

I want MY way.

Do you trust me?

Yes, but...

Are you ready to be blessed?

Yes, but only if it means having things MY way. I know how I want to be blessed. I have some great ideas...I could share them with You if You'd like.

Delight yourself in the Lord and He will give you the desires of your heart.

That's a trick verse. If I'm delighting myself in You then Your desires will become my desires. You will give me what I want but only because what I want has become what You want. But I still want what I want.

Humble Yourself and the Lord will lift You up in due time.

Give You EVERYTHING? My dreams, too? My plans, my hopes? Lord, I'm sorta attached to them. They're MINE. I give you my time. I share my talents. I tithe. I can even up it to 11% if You need me to.

I don't NEED anything from you. I just need you.

But Lord, they're MY dreams, MY hopes. What will you do with them? Will you still give me what I want? Or maybe You gave me my desires, my wishes, dreams and hopes. Maybe they were Yours all along.

There's only one way to find out.

Wait, was that a yes or a no?

Do you trust me? Am I only your God when life is good?

No, I guess not.

Do you trust me? Are you ready to be blessed?

I feel like this world wants to have its way with me. I'm so tired. I want to give up, and just let it win.

You're fighting me but I'm fighting for you. You're mine. I'm jealous for you. Take my hand. The world will not win...Are you ready to be blessed?

God's ways are higher than ours. He has His eyes on the entire picture while you and I are focused on just our one piece of the six-billion-plus piece puzzle. Despite His super-busy schedule, He would still leave it all in a flash—His throne, His deity, His authority and unnecessarily trade all of it for the bumps and bruises that accompany this life so that He could tell you face-to-face that you are not alone. Wait! He's already done that. Even if we don't get our way, we will never be alone.

Awhile back Clint was talking to the teens about following Christ the way that Christ deserves to be followed. Then my endearing, spirit-filled, genius idiot said,

"It's gonna be hard—but God is harder."

I liked the quote so much I typed it up, printed it out and hung it in the youth room where it has safely stayed ever since. Two days ago I *randomly* ran in there to make a phone call and that poster was there, hanging right above the phone, staring at me, reminding me that my God is tougher than any challenge I will ever face.

Are you strong enough to let go and trust Him? To worship even if you never get your way? To see the goodness of God shining through your darkness? Follow. Obey. Love. Go. There is no disclaimer that says, "Only when you feel like it."

Jesus wasn't all like, "Yipppeeee!" singing and dancing and skipping His way to the cross. He didn't want to die on a cross (Luke 22:42). He loved us so much that He *endured* the cross even though He didn't really *feel like it* and we definitely didn't deserve it. God gave us all of Himself. We were wounded dogs, snarling, hissing, gnashing our teeth and shouting "Crucify Him! Crucify Him!" to the only man in heaven or on earth or under the earth that knew what it would take to set us free and grant us the peace, joy, hope and love that our hearts were longing for.

We owed Him everything *before* He gave His life for us; now that He's gone and died in our place there is no way we will ever be able to tip the scales in our favor. So it's a really good thing then, wouldn't you agree, that our God is not a god of disclaimers? You can only get to heaven if... God doesn't play that way. Neither should we. I'll only follow You if... Come now, don't you think God deserves more than stale leftovers?

Right now you may not feel like you have much more than that to offer Him, but you do. Raise your hands above your head and tell God that you still love Him, that you know He still sees you and that you know He is worthy of your praise no matter what happens… and don't feel like you need to sing and dance and skip your way to that cross. Praising God when praising Him is hardest is the true meaning of a sacrifice of praise (Hosea 6:6, Matthew 9:13).

I don't know what the future holds for any of us. Even though this book is coming to an end, our stories will continue to be written one character at a time. Write with flavor. Write with passion. Better yet, if you want to be freaked out most of the time, put the pen in the Author's hands. He is, after all, the author of the greatest action-suspense-love story ever written.

Youth Director Sam
Comin' At You Live-ish:

You and I are going on a trip together. Right now. I'm a cheap date, promise. Take me to your favorite camp, retreat center, vacation spot, sanctuary or pub—the place where you feel most at peace. I made us a soundtrack for our roadtrip. Among others, five songs that have spoken to me over the last few months are "Praise You in This Storm" by Casting Crowns, "By Your Side" by Tenth Avenue North, "What Faith Can Do," by Kutless, "Held," by Natalie Grant and "The Desert Song" by Hillsong. (Prepare to cry quite a bit if you chose to youtube.com them for our imaginary getaway.)

There are other women with us on our getaway—hundreds of women who have lived through the same tragedy as you and me. Throughout the retreat we'll play crazy games with eggs and hula-hoops and we'll laugh our heads off, of course. We'll sing beautiful harmonies around the campfire—in the middle of your local pub—and we'll eat chocolate galore without gaining an inch around our waists. This is the *best retreat ever!*

Our sanctuary is a magical place where the sunset hangs in the sky quite a bit longer than you remember. The sky is rich with velvet violets and orange sherbets as the sun dangles just above the horizon with enough light to see our journals in front of us. We are near each other but alone as we lose ourselves to our private thoughts. The task we've been given is called "Letter to Self." We have been instructed to vent to, inspire, encourage and admonish our future selves. Hopes, dreams, feelings, fears, prayer requests—these are all things you write to yourself about.

Date: _____

Dear

_____
_____
_____
_____
_____
_____
_____
_____
_____
_____
_____
_____
_____
_____
_____
_____
_____
_____
_____

Your hand is shaking with sorrow and as you try to read over what you have just written, you find that between the tear-blurred vision and the sun dropping behind the horizon your attempt is futile. The dark sky amplifies the hopelessness you feel inside and your pen drops to the ground as you begin to sob.

Moments later the blue-collar hand of a close friend engulfs yours in His. At first it doesn't register with you that it should be too dark to see His hand. The first thing you wonder is how a man weaseled his way into a *woman's* retreat. Your eyebrows nearly scrunch into a perplexed expression until you look once again at His mocha-colored hands and see the scars at His wrists. Your eyes dart up to the man's face and dark, almond eyes stare back at you with peace, joy, hope and love.

The night shines as day to you while you sit in His presence. You tell Him everything that is on your heart and He shares His with you. "No eye has seen, nor ear has heard, nor the heart of man conceived, What God has prepared for those who love Him" (1 Corinthians 2:9). "I have come that you may have life and have it to the full" (John 10:10). "Do not let your heart be troubled. Trust the Father. Trust me" (John 14:1). "If you love me, you will obey what I command" (John 14:15).

Hours, days, months, you aren't entirely sure how long you spent in His presence. You just know that you never want to leave. Jesus laughs at your thoughts. They are no secret to Him. "You can take me with you," He reasons, as if it were not the obvious answer, but the *only* answer. "You can take me with you. It's where I'm meant to be."

As you take the first steps of your new adventure you wonder if He is matching your stride or if it is the other way around. Your legs are stronger, you notice, and your heart as well. Your sideward glance takes in the soldier walking beside you. You sense that you should feel like a burden, a disappointment to Him, but you don't. You don't deserve Him and yet, in the same heartbeat, you realize that He absolutely adores you and there is nowhere else in heaven or on earth or under the earth that He would rather be.

Samantha Evans

Lord Jesus, I pray for the woman reading this book. I pray that you would bless her and that she would not be able to doubt Your presence in her life. I ask Father, that you would see her God-given dreams fulfilled and speak to her heart the way that only You can. She needs you, Father. Holy Spirit be her peace and comfort, her deep and satisfying breath. Walk with her. Guide her. Love her, protect her, Your child. But above all, Father, I ask that Your will be done in her life and that she will trust You always no matter what happens. In your Holy Name I pray. Let it be so.

Appendix 1

I Like to Call This Appendix,
"Continued Ministry Connections"
OR...
"Youth Director Sam Comin' At
You More Live Than Live-ish"

I like to talk. You know this. And ministering to other people, helping them to experience the love, power and passion of Jesus Christ, is an honor that brings me great joy. It would be my pleasure to come share my testimony with you at your local church or women's retreat. Having been in ministry for over ten years, and with degrees in both Youth Ministry and Bible from Northwestern College in St. Paul, MN, I can easily adapt my testimony to any theme or Scripture passage you have in mind.

If you would like to learn more, here's how:

- ♥ Email me at loveletterstomiscarriedmoms@gmail.com
- ♥ Check out my website at loveletterstomiscarriedmoms.com
- ♥ You can also "Like" *Love Letters to Miscarried Moms* on Facebook

May the peace of God, which transcends all understanding, guard your hearts and minds in Christ Jesus.

Philippians 4:7

Appendix 2

Helpful Tips on How to Manage the Grieving

This short chapter is for those of you who may not know how to help or what to do for your friend, sister, daughter, niece (etc.) who has just miscarried her child and whose world has been turned upside-down. My suggestion: take a few minutes to read this chapter before you pass the book on. My words are just advice, not magic, so feel free to take or leave anything I have to say…

When I was in college I wrote a "book" called "Helpful Tips on How to Manage a Sam." It was mostly a joke. Some friends kidded that I should come with a manual, so I wrote one. The front and back cover were made of cardboard and the pages were hole-punched and tied together. In any event, for those of you who are reading this and have never experienced grief to this degree, I wanted to let you in on some insights that may make your efforts to love more effective.

The Verbals

For starters, don't pretend to understand what they are going through. Unless you have experienced the death of a child, sibling or spouse, you will not even come close to understanding her pain.

Six years ago my Aunt Thelma lost my Uncle Ron. Today we received a card from her in the mail. In the card she wrote, *"I've never experienced it myself, so I don't know how you feel, but I know it hurts."* At the end of the card she said, *"Of one thing I'm sure—Uncle Ron is holding and rocking your little one and will do so until you get there."*

Her words meant so much to me. Our loved ones are taking care of each other up in heaven. Your words don't have to be eloquent or lengthy, in fact there are no words that could possibly make the pain go away. "I love you" is not such a bad place to start. One of the things I have asked my fellow miscarried moms is, "What would you say to someone going through a miscarriage?"

Sandie's response was, "I love you and I'm in your corner." It's hard. You're teetering in such a delicate place because there are no words, but grieving mothers need to know that you care. You have a responsibility to your friends to love them. Just do your best.

The first week was definitely the hardest. I forced myself to leave the house and as I drove on this beautiful, bright sunny day I felt like there was one less person in the world. Numb. Detached. I got a text from Valerie, a mother-friend here in town who hasn't ever miscarried. Acts of love, love as a verb, have been the most impacting for me and Valerie was for me the hands and feet of Jesus.

In the text Valerie asked me, "What do you need right now?"

I responded. It was the first text I was trying to type since I'd dropped my phone into the fire and I thought about trying to explain that to her but it would have taken far too much effort. I'm not the best at texting as it is (yet another thing my teenagers laugh at me for) and texting with a phone that has been through the fire, so-to-speak, is not easy. Anyway, I managed, "I just need to stop crying right now."

"Can I bring you dinner?" I didn't respond. Partially because I was crying and partially because "I just need to stop crying right now" had taken far too much effort. She answered my text for me with "I'm bringing you dinner." Did she ever! Lasagna (that she baked in her own home before bringing it over), salad, dressing, garlic bread and chocolate ice cream for dessert. "So I [could] make one of my chocolate peanut butter shakes." If you can't cook, have a pizza sent to your friend's house. Something as simple as providing a meal (I lucked out with an extravagant one) will make all the difference in the world. Valerie sent a note with dinner that read (with God's beautiful, stick-it-to-me, don't-you-forget-it timing):

"God is with you...May His love be soothing. May His words bring you strength. May His promise fill your heart with His peace. With deepest sympathy to you at this time of sorrow. Sam and Clint, we love you both and are praying for you. God's love never fails! In Christ, Kyle and Valerie.

'I will not leave you. I will come to you' John 14:8.

I will never ever forget Valerie's kindness.

Also, flowers, cards or notes, though they make your friend cry, will be much appreciated. Two friends brought me flowers within the week. When they started to go bad, I pressed them in my journal and then covered them with plastic packaging tape so they would keep their color—it didn't work, but I tried. One of them, a memorial rose, was the last in Diana's garden this season.

Let me shift gears to talk about texting for a minute. We are a cyberspace generation and I would have to say that a majority of our communication is done through a keyboard or keypad. Grief cannot be text away and no one should try. If you *can* say anything nice, *say it*, don't type it. A miscarriage is a personal loss and deserves personal sympathy.

People said some very careless things to me that I wish they hadn't. Please choose your words carefully. Say what you mean; mean what you say—that applies here. Empty platitudes don't do the trick. For instance, if you say, "Maybe I'll stop by," please take the time to stop by. If you don't have time for a visit, that's alright—just don't *say* that you might. Also, if you do say something dumb, don't beat yourself too long. You are the batter up in an impossible, no-win situation.

I've heard people say that they are afraid to bring up what happened, to remind the grieving of the loss and cause sadness. This sounds almost logical, but as someone who is grieving, let me let you in on a grief-reality. My miscarriage happened nearly three weeks ago and there has not been a day that has gone by without me thinking about it. You wouldn't shock me with the news. It's on the forefront of my mind, anyway. And like my Aunt Mary Beth said, "there will be a day maybe a year or so from now when you realize that you didn't think about it at all that day. Some time will pass and all of a sudden you'll realize that you haven't thought about it for *three* or *four* days."

A year—that's a long time. And just when a mother thinks she's about to get over it she will run upon her initial due date, her baby's first birthday, and the time of the year that she had been pregnant. At some point, each grieving mother will feel sad because the world is moving on and forgetting about her pain. In those moments she will be really lonely for her child. You will move on *long* before she has, so, if you are still thinking about her miscarriage, chances are high that your mother-friend is as well.

It may vary from mother to mother, but I don't think that a "Hey, I saw such-and-such and it made me think of you. How have you been doing?" is a bad thing. It helps us to know that you still remember and still care.

The Non-Verbals

Ninety percent of how we communicate is NON-verbal, which says a great deal about body language and voice inflection, which are both in the non-verbal category. Verbal communication is words only. That's it. That is why sometimes communication is misconstrued via mediums such as text or email despite our best efforts to assimilate cyber body language. ☺ Smileys ;) Winks =0 Gasps and <3 Hearts only go so far. Ninety percent of communication is lost in translation.

Now, I'm really going to do my best to coach you through this without sounding like a Psychology book but it might be difficult. I want to mention is a term called "mirroring." This does not only go for people who are grieving, but people in general. Everyone has a different physical comfort level that varies greatly depending on whether or not the person is a relative or acquaintance and how that person is feeling.

Therefore, when someone is grieving (or not), study her facial expressions and gestures as you speak to one another. If she doesn't reach out her arms to hug you, please don't grab her and pull her into a hug! The week after I miscarried I did not want to be touched by many people. It was partly because I felt dirty and nasty with an excessive amount of blood still draining and partly because my emotional stability was hanging on by such a thin thread that I feared if someone hugged me or started crying I would fall to pieces, unable to be put back together again.

I had one friend once (before my miscarriage) that thought that because I was not in tears (about something else) that I was not responding the way that I should. Don't be that friend. Everyone grieves differently and unless she has fallen apart in your arms, please do your best to keep it together.

So, I was telling this woman, within the week that it happened, that I had miscarried and I physically put my arm out in the "Stop in the name of love" sort of fashion and firmly said, "I don't want to be hugged right now." She hugged me anyway! Needless to say, I was unhappy. Another couple turned my news into a group hug and I had to break free of them, much as I picture a superhero breaking free of his bounds. To them I said, "Okay, that's enough hugging."

One woman came into the office about a month afterward. She looked at me with these puppy eyes that were on the verge of tears and said, "I need to apologize to you."

"For what," I asked. *Oh no, not that.* I had been in a good mood; I was getting things done. At that moment the miscarriage was not at the forefront of my mind. She was not paying attention to me. All of a sudden I was holding this sobbing woman, rubbing her back and consoling her over my loss.

This may sound selfish to you but it is important to grasp. It's *her* grief. She's allowed to respond however she needs to. You need to respond however she needs you to. It's a one-way street.

Pay attention to her facial expressions. Cry when she's crying. Laugh when she's laughing. I know this may sound absurdly simple but it's really important to understand. Ask her questions that allow her to direct the tone of the conversation such as "How has your day been?" or "What have you been up to today?"

Most importantly for her, try to grasp that she is a mother who has lost her child. She was making plans for the future. She was coming up with names and trying to decide if her child would be athletic or artsy, spunky or subdued and whether or not he or she would have the brilliant looks of the mother or be stuck with Dad's ugly mug. Please, do not for a second think that because her child wasn't born, that the loss is somehow less severe, less painful or less tragic. I'm crying right now as I type this because I miss my baby so much. It wasn't just an embryo or a fetus. It was my child and it's gone now. I know that her heart is broken because mine is too. So I'm begging you, please be gentle with her. Her heart is so frail.

Most importantly for you, cut yourself some slack. When all is said and done and you are kicking yourself for saying or doing the wrong thing, just let it go. You love her; she knows this. And she loves you, too. Your mother-friend will appreciate your best efforts one day—maybe just not in the moment. And don't take anything she says personally. She's not exactly a picture of emotional clarity right now.

I know you love her. I know you'll be great, and, from my heart and hers, thank you so much for reading this and trying to understand where she's coming from. We appreciate it. ☺

Appendix 3

Meet the Cast

The Wonderful Women Who Have Helped Me Through My Grief

My Aunt Mary Beth is a nurse in Hinsdale, IL. She is the mother of Christy, Carissa, Catie (whose real name is Melissa but it's a long story for another book), Child of God, Cheryl, Child of God and Robert. Aunt Mary's first miscarriage was like mine, in the first trimester. Her second miscarriage, actually considered a still-birth, happened at five months.

My cousin Jennifer (Aka Jenny) is married to Jarred and is the mother of Jacob, Christiana (Tiny), Caroline (Chevelle), and Child of God. Though it would have been her fourth child, recovering from the loss has been a difficult journey for Jenny because she has felt in her heart that her family is missing one more person. Even before she was pregnant with Child of God, she would look at her three children and feel like she was missing one. "I'd turn around in the store and see three children and wonder why I felt like there should be more." Jenny miscarried around Thanksgiving of 2007. I remember hearing about it and thinking, *Oh, that's too bad.* Never in my life, could I have fathomed the pain that she was going through—until now.

This just in: Charlotte Mae, born July 30th, 2010, 9:25 am - 7lbs 14oz, 21 inches long. Jenny and Jared's Number 4.

My Aunt Diane is the mother of Child of God, Child of God and Daughter of God. Knowing our family, the other two were probably girls as well. There are fifteen cousins on my dad's side. Two of them are boys. I could take a guess on the color of their big, Dutch eyes, as well. Her favorite Sman-tha quote is, "Auntie Di, you have my eyes." I was young and thought I could have given Einstein a run for his money when I discovered that our eyes were the same color: a ring of brown around a ring of green.

Dr. Mary is my family doctor and OBGYN. She said that, looking back, she realizes that it wasn't the right time for her and her husband to have a baby. The miscarriage helped them begin to seriously evaluate lifestyle changes that would help them make room in their lives for a bigger family. For example, the job that she'd had at the time never would have allowed for her to raise her children. Dr. Mary is the mother of Child of God, Connor, Cameron and Elizabeth.

Erica is our church's Administrative Assistant. I have always marveled at the amount of patience and discernment she seems to have for the chaos that is our church at times. Her husband's name is Coe and she is the mother of Child of God, Payton and Cade, which I believe she would readily tell you, are the source of her unfathomable learned patience.

Lori has a sign in her house that reads: "There are four seasons in this house: Winter, Spring, Summer and Football." Lori is the wife of Mike and mother of Child of God, Steven (who is currently in Japan with the Navy), Alex and Sam. Her life is crazy busy but she loves what she does and would have it no other way. The first and second day after I miscarried, she made time for me which I now realize, coming from Lori, was a very special gift.

My friend Dia is the mother of Child of God, Iollia, Naida, Child of God, Child of God, Malinna, Child of God and Enarra (born during this book's editing process). She and her husband, Dana, good friends of ours, cleverly nicknamed our child Little Clam. It is a combination of Clint and Sam. Following our miscarriage Dana ministered to Clint and Dia to me. They knew what we were going through.

My friend Monica married Nat when she was nineteen and has basically been pregnant ever since. She's twenty-nine now and her children are Addison, Christian, Beth (Bethy), Titus, Sidney, Cadence, Child of God and Eva. Eight in ten years, in case you're counting on your fingers—and she has one on the way. There is a *lot* of energy in that household. Most of it, in my humble opinion, comes from Titus, who, when he was four, ran up to me, flexed his four-year-old biceps and said, very definitively, "I'm a *strong* little buddy. My Tigger says so." When he was five he stuck rubber handled pliers into the electrical outlet and yelled, "Mommy, look! Fireworks!" Monica tried to scold him but she was laughing too hard. I want that energy in my life…maybe not eight kids worth of energy, but now that I have been pregnant I realize that our house is emptier than it used to be.

Misty has a beautiful heart and a beautiful voice. The day I was pregnant (before I peed on the stick) she learned that I was the same age as her oldest son and announced that she would be my surrogate mom. The day I miscarried she had just left for vacation but promised that when she got back home she would spoil me rotten. She's kept her promise. When my mom expressed the wish that she could be close to me in this time, I told her about Misty and she said, "Oh, good, I'm glad. That makes me feel better." Misty is the wife of Jeff and mother of Child of God, Steven, Jarred and Julian.

Dr. Gwen is a longtime family friend. She once examined me in the men's Sunday school classroom one Sunday after church when I was sick and had no insurance. She and her husband Mike go back as far as my memories do. Mike and Gwen are the parents of Matt, Child of God and Child of God. I remember when Matt was born. He's now graduated from Illinois Wesleyan. This makes me feel very old.

Sandie is the mother of Son and Daughter of God, Son of God and Son of God. We became instant friends when we learned that we had the same birthday. Sandie is like a cross between Betty Crocker and McGuiver. The woman can do anything she sets her mind to doing and has the tenacity required to pull it off, which made not being able to have children really hard on her. "Why am I not good enough?" she questioned of herself. It doesn't mean that she didn't give it everything she had. Sandie's heart stopped for each of her three stillborn deliveries. After the third time they resuscitated her she decided to raise the white flag.

Lona is the mother of Andrew, Aaron, Arika, and twins Son of God and Daughter of God. Lona is a silent hero who works diligently behind the scenes and is cozy there. She isn't a huge fan of public accolades, which is why this paragraph, accessible to people all across the globe, makes me smile. Lona's children, grandchildren, church, community, students and friends are all blessed because of her good deeds. She is a beautiful reminder to me that people can make a significant difference in this world without having to be gushy, showy, "yaza, yaza" about it. So cheers, accolades and yaza yazas to Lona, who would never seek them for herself.

The more I talk about it with people, the more other women approach me to let me know that they have experienced the same thing. As I spoke to Sandie, I learned that her mother also had a few miscarriages—essentially every other child. One was a twin that she lost at seven months, while carrying the other to full term. My friend Annie is the mother of two beautiful girls with another on the way. Her miscarriage happened before this last pregnancy and happened while she was at the hospital with a friend of hers who was in labor. My friend Sonia was in the National Guard. She and her boyfriend were in the same company and she got pregnant and miscarried while in Iraq.

Grandma Lewis was the mother of Edward John, Ruth, Child of God, Thelma, Diane, Child of God, Mary Beth and Edward James. She had fifteen grandchildren and seventeen great-grandchildren, with three on the way, when she passed away at the beginning of December, 2010. She was greeted in heaven by her husband, son, son-in-law and two children she'd never met, five grandchildren and four great-grandchildren.

On her last day, I asked Aunt Mary Beth to pass on a message for me. "Please tell Grandma that I was looking forward to seeing her at Christmastime, but that I won't hold it against her if she decides that she has better plans. And please ask her to rock my babies for me." Aunt Mary told me that when she passed along the message to Grandma, who was unresponsive by that point, Grandma squeezed her hand in acknowledgement. Aunt Mary also assured the family that as Grandma moved from one life to the next, the room was filled with the peace that passes all understanding (Philippians 4:7).

Now the moments that she spent with me on the phone are priceless—her Christmas gift, her legacy to me.

All of our stories are different. The loss is the same. You will see their names pop up off and on throughout this book because these are the women who laughed when I laughed and wept when I wept. They celebrated the joy of my pregnancies and hurt with me through the loss of my children.